Property Investment

How to fund your retirement with a buy-to-let property pension

DAWN BROOKES

Published by DAWN BROOKES PUBLISHING
www.dawnbrookespublishing.com
Kindle Edition 2017
Paperback Edition 2017
ISBN: 978-0-9955561-6-4
Copyright © DAWN BROOKES 2017

Cover Design by Janet Dado
Front cover image: ©punghi/fotolia images

Property Investment

How to fund your retirement with a buy-to-let property pension

DAWN BROOKES PUBLISHING
www.dawnbrookespublishing.com

To my mum for teaching me what was important in life

Claim Your *FREE* Bonus

As a thank you for reading this book, I have put together a bonus for you to claim for FREE. Sign up to gain instant access to the bonus at: http://www.buytoletinfo.com/property-hotspots/

Bonus

Quick-start Guide to UK hotspots for buy to let property in 2017

This report looks at a number of property hotspots with thriving buy to let investment areas throughout the United Kingdom. Included in the report is an area for speculative investment.

To access the report for free please go to http://www.buytoletinfo.com/property-hotspots/

Password to access: Bonus

Introduction

Anyone Can Invest in Property

Before we launch into the exciting world of property investment, let me tell you a little bit about myself. I spent thirty-nine years working in the National Health Service in England as my day job. I loved my job most of the time and I am even writing a series of memoirs about it. Working in the NHS though, I was never going to have a lot of was money. I had enough to live on and enough to get a mortgage, and the NHS offers (or did offer) a good pension scheme which was probably one of the only perks.

I have a lot of friends and acquaintances who have owned by-to-let property and I even managed rental property for friends for a while. I developed knowledge of the process but didn't ever consider it as something I would do until about seven years ago. You could say I had a 'light bulb' moment! I was growing tired of the stress and strain of working full time in the NHS and was probably approaching burnout – does this sound familiar? Anyway, suddenly I realised that property investment was something that could fund an earlier retirement (or semi-retirement) and even free me from the day job if I went about it in a serious way.

From that moment, I read everything I could about the process, watched *Homes under the Hammer* every day, and after researching for about eighteen months decided to take the plunge. I had always been good at negotiating; I learned the skill on a trip to Asia in my early twenties. The property market was still reeling from the last recession when I invested in my first property, which I bought for £97,000 even though it was on the market for £120,000. It had been on the market for a long time and I arrived when the seller had finally had enough of waiting to sell and wanted to get rid of it. The property was in need of full refurbishment and didn't have gas central heating. The refurbishment cost £12,000, including installing gas central heating. Upon completion of the two months of work, the property was already worth £125,000. Needless to say, I didn't sell the property; instead, I rented it out and, with the first experience under my belt, I began to build a property portfolio.

I have loved every minute of it so far and, although I initially used an agent, I now manage all the properties myself. I have been fortunate enough not to have any void periods and have found excellent tenants because of a rigid screening process that I apply. There is no reason why you cannot do what I have done and be in a position to fund your retirement in the near or more distant future. As long as you pay due diligence to the process and take a well-informed approach, you can develop a property portfolio from scratch. I hope that you find this book useful and that it provides you with enough information and motivation to get started.

Retire Well

If I were to ask myself what are the key things I would want in retirement it would be good health, happiness and financial security. The reason I add financial security apart from the obvious is that I would want the ability to enjoy my leisure time and not have to worry about whether I could afford the next holiday or the next car. Anything else is a bonus.

3

This book is about developing financial security in retirement through property investment, but we all need to remind ourselves that money isn't everything. I can't give you health or happiness. However, hopefully by reading this book, I can offer you some skills that will enable you to build up a property portfolio and have financial security in retirement. Some skills developed through the discipline needed to stay healthy are going to help us to stay financially secure. The one thing that many people lack today is discipline – by this, I mean self-discipline. The world has changed so much and debt has become so easy to accumulate; the majority of people have debts well into the tens of thousands of pounds, not counting their mortgage debt. This cannot be good: we need to develop a healthy respect for money so that we can use it wisely and instead of blowing it all now, we need to plan ahead. I am not being a kill-joy; of course, we want to enjoy ourselves too. We will consider elements of debt in this book and contrast good debt with bad debt.

An Ipsos MORI poll conducted in 1999 found that 25 million adults had little or no savings. I think if the same poll were conducted today it might be even worse. We have a 'no savings' generation out there. Partly this could be blamed on university fees and low interest rates, but not all. Government borrowing hardly sets a good example. This book does not aim to put the world to rights but we do need to sensibly invest in our futures in order to retire well.

Retirement for many people means an opportunity to experience some great things, such as taking the holiday of a lifetime, spending more time with family, friends and grandchildren, and generally having more leisure time. Leisure activities will be more readily available to us if we have more money as well as more time. We may even achieve lifetime ambitions, such as writing a book, starting a small business or going to university. Remember that we are living longer and the opportunities available to us now are huge if we take the time to think about what we would like to do with our time in retirement.

Financial Security

Whilst I have already stated that money isn't everything, a lack of money is horrible. When thinking about retirement, we don't want to be thinking about how on earth we are going to survive. We don't want to be worrying about bills or where the next meal will come from. We need to feel that if a fridge or a car goes wrong, we will be able to get it fixed or replaced without having to forego the next holiday. One thing is sure: the State Pension is unlikely to be enough to provide the security we need in retirement and we don't really want to be dependent on benefits.

Ideally, when we retire we want to be mortgage-free, living in our own homes and have enough income coming in to provide for the lifestyle that we had hoped for before retiring. Let's take a look at how investing in even a small property portfolio can provide us with the lifestyle we would like for many years to come. It may be that you have a work pension to rely on as well as the state pension and this is a good thing too. Whether it is enough, however, is another matter.

Chapter 1

Pensions

The biggest challenge facing society and each of us individually is that we are living longer and, at present as a result, will be retired for longer. One of the major concerns for the government and for us as individuals is how to fund retirement. There are other challenges which include funding healthcare for the future, but that is not what this book is about. It is great that we are living longer and I read a headline recently that said 90 is the new life expectancy. As stated in the previous chapter, we want to be as healthy, happy and financially secure as possible in retirement.

People who don't invest for retirement may find that they cannot afford to do the things they had wanted to and may even struggle to put food on the table.

Before going into detail about how to invest in property as part of your pension plan, we need to take a look at the other pensions that will be available to you.

State Pension

Firstly, there is no guarantee that the State Pension will still be around in the future, although we hope that it will be. The state pension age will continue to rise over the next twenty years and the goalposts are likely to keep moving.

There are three forms of State Pension available these are:

- Old rules 1 – apply to men born before 6th April 1951 and women born before 6th April 1953 and you reached state pension age before 6th April 2016
- Old rules 2 – apply to men born before 6th April 1945 and women born before 6th April 1950

- New state pension – applies to men born on or after 6th April 1951 and women born on or after 6th April 1953

Old Rules 1 State Pension

The maximum amount paid at the time of writing is £119.30 per week but this is increased annually. In order to qualify for the maximum amount a person needs to have 30 full years' eligible contributions. You can get your pension statement estimation here or, if reading a physical version of this book you can go the pensions section at https://www.gov.uk/state-pension/overview. The pension is paid weekly.

There is a calculation set by which this pension is increased year on year and details of this can be found on the government website.

Old Rules 2 State Pension

The qualifying years are higher for both men (44 years for full pension and 11 years for any) and women (39 years for full and 10 years for any) and those who have not made eligible payments are not entitled to any state pension at all.

A state pension is not paid automatically but the pensions department should write approximately four months before retirement age to let people know how to claim. A person can still work after receiving the pension but it could be taxable if over the minimum allowance that can be earned before tax.

New State Pension

The maximum amount paid at the time of writing is £155.65 per week; the pension is paid four weekly in arrears. In order to qualify for any pension under the new rules a person needs to have paid 10 years eligible contributions. For people who began paying National Insurance after 6th April 2016 they will need to have 35 eligible years in order to qualify for the full pension.

If you live in Scotland, Wales or Northern Ireland you will be entitled to a bus pass at the age of sixty, but if you live in England you have to wait until your retirement age.

There are various scenarios relating to marriage and civil partnerships and inheritance; details can be found on the government website for pensions as stated above.

State Pension age

This is a moving feast at the moment but I think you can assume that if you are under 30 years old you will likely have to work until you are at least 70 years old before you can claim.

Current State of Affairs

- If you are 65 up to end November 2018 then you will retire at 65
- Retirement age increases to 66 between December 2018 & October 2020
- Retirement age increases to 67 from April 2018
- Retirement age increases to 68 from April 2046 (new proposals to increase this to age 70 - watch this space)

The truth of the matter is that we are living longer and therefore would live a lot longer into retirement than previously, which is unaffordable and so the State Pension age could keep increasing more rapidly than currently set out if life expectancy continues to increase.

Conclusion

One thing is certain: at whatever age you are allowed to claim your state pension, living a good life in retirement is not going to be possible on the State Pension alone. It might pay a few bills but it is hardly going to enable you to do all the things you have wanted to do when you finally give up work.

Private Pensions

Work-based Pension

There has been a lot in the press recently about work-based pensions. The government now requires every employer to offer a work-based pension, although employees can opt out. If you don't opt out you are automatically enrolled and a certain amount of money will be deducted from your salary each month. This also attracts tax relief and your employer has to contribute money too which is a good thing. Whilst this is great in many ways, the amount you receive in retirement will depend on how much you earn and how your money is invested over the time that you contribute. Contributing to a pension does make sense and at least you will be entitled to something at the end of it which is better than not having a pension at all.

Many pension plans do not pay out a good return on investment as bitter experience has told many, but if you are not going to do anything else to invest for the future, they are a necessary evil and, as I said before, your employer contributes too!

Defined Benefit (final salary)

These are excellent pension schemes as they are calculated on a percentage of the employee's final or average salary. They are often referred to as final salary pension schemes. The employee pays into the scheme alongside the employer; the money goes into a pension fund and the employee receives a generous pension at the end based on their final few years' income. These schemes are expensive for employers as they have to find the money to pay the pensions for the life of the recipient. The pensions also rise with inflation each year.

They are mainly available for public sector workers such as nurses, doctors, teachers and many others. They have now been replaced by the majority of employers due to the costs to the employer. Some people who are due to retire in the near future will still benefit from such schemes. The government is also offering modified schemes to public sector workers and is actively encouraging staff to move into new schemes that will cost the employer less in the long term. They have now been replaced in companies by Defined Contribution Schemes.

Defined Contribution

These schemes mean that the employee and the employer contribute a certain percentage of salary each month which is paid into a pension fund. The fund is invested by a company. In this case, however, the benefit at the end is not known because it will depend on how the money is invested and what it is worth in the future. The employee in this case is not sure of how much they will receive in retirement.

Features of Defined Contribution

Size and number of contributions, how it is invested.

Growth

Most growth inside the pension is tax free, so if you contribute for forty years with a decent growth this will provide a decent pension at the end of the term. Growth depends on the performance of the stock market. Stock market growth is unsteady: it can be conservative, average or fast growing. The better the growth rate, the better the pension in the end.

How long it is allowed to grow

The longer the contribution term, the better the pay-out as this allows for compounding of interest.

Charges and costs over the plan term

At retirement you have to purchase an annuity from the company holding the fund or take income drawdown once you have released a tax free lump sum. These generally pay very poorly and are often below £3,500 per year, even if you have around £100,000 in the fund at retirement. The more money you accumulate in the fund, the better the pension return will be.

What to do with pension

Annuities

Most people would have had the option to buy an annuity or take income drawdown. Annuities have been very low in recent years and many people have been extremely disappointed with the payments. They do, however, provide a regular taxable income for life. The amount you get from an annuity very much depends on the amount of income in your pension fund at retirement and they do take into account lifestyle factors. You may actually get more money if you are a smoker as your life expectancy is reduced.

Income Drawdown

This means you can keep the money invested in the fund and draw income from it. The amount that can be drawn is capped.

Changes from 2015

George Osborne, the previous Chancellor, stated in a 'headline' grabbing statement that the pension changes occurring from 2015 would be 'the most radical changes to pensions in almost a century'. Many experts think that the changes to pensions by the then Chancellor were irresponsible and may have caused people to withdraw and spend their pension funds without investing for the future. The changes, though, do offer more flexibility to individuals. From the age of 55 a person can access a part or their entire pension fund.

The rule changes do not affect Defined Benefit, known as Final salary pension schemes, but they do affect defined contribution schemes. The government, however, is going to offer people in final salary schemes the option to transfer into a defined contribution scheme basically because they know that the final salary schemes offer great rates for employees. Most people would advise against this move, but obviously, if it affects you, seek financial advice. For many people the only options on retirement or when they took their lump sums out of a pension scheme were to buy an annuity or to take income drawdown. There have been some changes to both annuity rules and drawdown's, so seek financial advice if you intend to take either of these options.

Cashing in pension

The changes have altered from releasing a 25% tax free lump sum to the option of releasing the whole amount of pension. Only 25% is tax free, while the remaining amount is taxable income. The fear is that some people will withdraw the whole amount, spend it and not have any retirement income. Clearly this option does not make sense, but it has happened in many cases.

In terms of investing in property this presents an opportunity for people who would prefer to have more control over where their money is invested and that is what this book is about.

Example 1

£320,000 pension pot
25% tax free = £80,000

Any additional withdrawal is taxable: in this case a further £240,000 could be withdrawn in part or as a whole but the tax bill would be hefty with the majority of the income falling into the higher rate tax band.

Example 2

£120,000 in pension pot
25% tax free = £30,000

The remaining £90,000 is taxable

Most people are likely to take the 25% and use the remaining amount to buy an annuity or take income drawdown. Some people will withdraw the money and spend it or pay off their home mortgage and some may use the money to invest in buy-to-let property. I am not advising anyone to do this but, if you do, then investing in property rather than spending it on an annuity may make more sense.

Seek financial advice, but remember that financial advisors earn commission from you investing in annuities but not if you invest in property.

Example Annuity versus Buy-to-Let Property Investment

£90,000 annuity likely to offer annual income of between £2,500 and £3,000 (estimated) for life.

If you were to withdraw £90,000 and pay tax on that amount, you would be left with approximately £72,000 (depending on other income) to invest in property whilst keeping your tax free sum of £30,000 to spend.

The £72,000, if it were invested in property could buy one to three properties (with mortgages) with a potential return on investment of around £3,000 per property after costs, plus capital growth. This means that you could earn at least the same and potentially three times the amount gained from buying an annuity – and whereas an annuity would provide no further growth, property would still be growing your money year on year through capital growth. You can see why property investment remains a healthy option for many people.

Self Employed & Opting Out of Auto-enrolment

If you are self employed, you may not be investing in a pension scheme at all unless you have actively sought to do so. Also, if you are employed and choose to opt out of auto-enrolment into a work-based pension scheme you will not have a private pension in retirement. In both instances, property investment would be an ideal way of investing for the future and worth considering.

As previously stated, it is unlikely that a State Pension alone is going to fund a financially secure retirement, so not investing in any form of pension doesn't make financial sense. By investing in property you will be ensuring that you have something to fall back on in the future.

Conclusion

This chapter is not meant to be an exhaustive discussion of pensions, but provides instead an overview for you to research a bit more. The exciting thing about the government pension changes in terms of investing in property is that if you do want to invest in property for a pension then you have every opportunity to do so.

Chapter 2

Property as a Pension

In spite of the government making it more difficult for people to invest in property through extra stamp duty, tax and legislative changes, property is still a great way to invest money. Many investment companies advise against investing in property but you have to take into account that they may have ulterior motives. They will not make money if you invest in property instead of annuities, etc. You do need to understand that investing in property comes with responsibilities though, for example property management, but these can be outsourced to letting agents. This plan will work for you whether you want to retire completely or reduce your hours as you grow older.

Demand for property

The demand for property is still outstripping supply and as long as this continues property will always be a good investment. We know that there is a property shortage and more people renting now than in previous years. These are not all first-time buyers who can't get on the property ladder as the government would have us believe. In fact, many people rent due to relationship breakups. Students also make up a large part of the rental market, as do people on benefits.

Don't take too much notice of people who say that investing in property is dead and that investing in property is too risky. Of course, you should pay due diligence to the market and weigh up the financial implications prior to investing as you would for any major investment.

Many of the people who advise against investing in property are stock brokers who want to take your money and make themselves very rich through commission and fees. Rarely do you become rich from other people investing your money in the stock market. That doesn't mean I'm against stocks and shares: I own stocks and shares, and I have a nice 25% capital growth from investing myself with the advice of a mentor who I pay. It's not my favourite form of investment, though, and dividend returns are nowhere near the return of rent from property. I prefer property and I'm passionate about property in a way that I could never be about investing in stocks and shares. I love investing in property and I think it's because it is tangible and it makes sense that people will always need homes.

One of the many reasons people do invest in property is that as you can see what you are buying hopefully you better understand the market. It is difficult to understand the stock market as you don't invest in one stock; instead, you invest in numerous stocks, thereby spreading your risk but it makes it more difficult to understand the companies you are investing in.

If you consider human needs, we all need food and shelter. I wish I had started investing 20 years ago as I started investing in my 50s. I am just happy that I have started and as I have invested for a healthy pension I can truly recommend this form of investment with the proviso that you invest within your means.

If you can own as many properties as possible by the time you retire you will have a very decent pension. You can aim to own them outright by the time you retire or continue with interest only mortgages into your 70s. If the latter frightens you aim to start as soon as possible: the younger the better with the aim of owning outright by the time you need the retirement income. It is not necessary to own them outright, though: investing, and how you invest, will depend on your overall goals.

The number of properties required will depend on where you live, what your salary is now and the amount of income you would like to retire on. In general, three to four rental properties plus your own home should be enough to provide a steady income for life. It is more difficult in the current climate to take out a buy-to-let repayment mortgage due to punitive affordability criteria being applied by lenders but it is still possible and we will discuss how to do this in chapter 4.

Example of how it might work for you

Here is an example of a person with a salary of £48,000 per year who would like to continue earning that amount (in principle) in retirement. Firstly, deduct tax then mortgage payments from the salary because you will be mortgage free.

£48,000 – tax free allowance of £11,500 = £36,500

Taxable Income £36,500

Basic rate tax deducted £7,300

Tax free allowance added £11,500

Total Income £40,700

Mortgage Payments per annum deducted assuming £850 per month = £10,200

This leaves £30,500 per annum disposable income minus bills

From the example above you would need to earn £30,500 after tax in retirement to be in the same position as you were when working. I have not included the State Pension as you may want to retire before State retirement age. In the example in Table 2.1 below I show how owning five rental properties in different price bands can earn you the same amount of disposable income in retirement as a salary of £48,000 per annum would have done during working life while paying a mortgage. This is a fair assumption as most people have mortgages on their own homes up to retirement. The example also assumes that your own home and all of your rental properties will be mortgage free by the time you retire. Not to worry if they are not mortgage free but you will need more properties to produce the same amount of income. If your working salary is lower and you only want to earn a similar income in retirement you would need fewer properties.

If your salary is much higher and you live in a more expensive part of the country you may well need fewer properties to provide a good income and you may well have a personal pension too. I can't provide examples for every scenario but I am sure that you can work out what you need using the principle here. We will go into more detail throughout this book.

The table has not included capital gains which would likely provide you with large lump sums of money should you wish to take money out of one or all of the properties subject to capital gains tax. I have assumed a basic rate tax payer with other income providing a tax free allowance. It is impossible to create a table for every part of the United Kingdom because property and rental prices differ so markedly. It is possible; however, to estimate for one particular area and in the example shown here the prices apply to the East Midlands of England.

There are areas where property prices will be much lower and you will be able to own more properties with equivalent or lower rental income and then there are areas like London where property prices are so high, it might be difficult (but not impossible) to get started. If you did own properties in London, you would need fewer properties to achieve this type of income if you have held them for a long time. If you were to buy property in London now though, the yields tend to be less than 3% as the London rental market is relatively flat.

	Rental Property 1	Rental Property 2	Property 3	Property 4	Property 5
Rental income	£730 per month	£575	£550	£550	£1,200
Costs	£100	£100	£100	£100	£100
Taxable income	£7,760	£5,900	£5,600	£5,600	£13,400
Tax	£1,552	£1,180	£1,120	£1,200	£2,680
Income to spend	£6,208	£4,720	£4,480	£4,480	£10,720
	£30,608 Disposable income				

Table 2.1 Potential income generation from five properties in the East Midlands

In the example shown above, five properties in addition to your own home would be enough to fund a retirement income equivalent to that of £48,000 per annum when you are mortgage free. If you need to continue with interest only mortgages you would need to own more properties for that amount of income. In Table 2.2 I have set out what this might look like if you only held the four properties above but with mortgages, still assuming that you will have paid off your home mortgage by the time you retire. Yield is discussed in detail in chapter 10.

	Rental Property 1	Rental Property 2	Property 3	Property 4	Property 5
Rental income	£730 per month	£575	£550	£550	£1.200
Costs	(£100)	(£100)	£100	(£100)	(£100)
Taxable income	£7,760	£5,900	£5,600	£5,600	£13,400
Tax	£1,552	£1,180	£11,200	£1,120	£2,680
Mortgage Interest	(£373)	(£168)	(£165)	(£165)	(£495)
Tax allowance 2020 @ 20%	£895.20	£403.20	£396	£396	£1,188
Income to spend	£2,627.20	£3,107.20	£2,896	£2,896	£5,968
	£17,494.40 Disposable Income				

Table 2.2 Potential income from four properties with mortgages

In the example above I have made the assumption that these mortgages are in place after the government has reduced the total tax relief on mortgage interest to 20% per annum and that profits are calculated without mortgage interest being applied initially. These changes come into effect in 2020 and the first phase of change is happening in the current tax year, 2017 – 2018. Claim your free copy of examples of the four year implementation by going to my website at http://www.buytoletinfo.com. I have also assumed that you will be a basic rate taxpayer at retirement, if any of your income falls into the higher rate tax band, then you will either need to lower your income or hold more properties.

If you think this looks bad, don't forget that on top of this income you will receive a State Pension and that the tenants are paying your mortgage. The only finance you need to come up with is that required to buy the property in the first place, which you will do prior to retirement. We will look at ways to increase your portfolio in more detail in chapter 8.

Inflation

You would be right in assuming that inflation and cost of living rises will affect the value of the income shown in these examples. Remember that this works in both positive and negative ways. The positive is that the amount you will owe on an interest only mortgage will also be worth less in the future, making interest only mortgages more attractive. Another positive is that rents will also increase over time and the figures shown in the examples will be higher so that it should all balance itself out.

A recent estimation for earning a pension of £20,000 in retirement suggested that you needed to invest between £250 and £860 per month into a defined contribution scheme (depending on the age at which you start) and that is just to achieve £12,000 annuity plus your state pension of £8,000. For some people that means investing between 40-50% of salary if starting at a later age. Women also have to invest more because they live longer. I know where I would rather put my money! It is a plus if you have a work-based pension as well as a property portfolio.

Bank of England Chief Economist Gave Property a Thumbs Up

Before you think that you can't invest in property because you don't have enough money, read the rest of this book to look at how you build up a property portfolio with just your first property deposit coming out of your own pocket. If that doesn't convince you, even the Bank of England's Chief Economist, Andy Haldane, suggested that Residential Property beats pensions for investment planning for retirement. The reason for this is that historically house prices rise and continue to do so, and because of a nationwide property shortage, there is more demand than supply. This is sensible economics: whenever demand outstrips supply, prices continue to rise both in terms of property price and rental income. Obviously, there are times when property prices fall but they have always recovered and risen over time. None of us know what the future holds, but investment in the stock market (which is where your pension money goes) is hardly a fail-safe.

So now that we have seen that investing in property can provide or at least support retirement income let's take a look at how to invest in the first place and what sort of plan makes sense for using a property portfolio for pension investment.

Chapter 3

Money Needed

If you have decided to invest in property you will usually need a minimum of a 25% deposit plus a few other purchasing expenses in order to buy the first rental property. The more deposit you have, the better the interest rate but interest rates generally fall in increments as follows:

- Deposit 20% = 80% Loan to Value (LTV), you may find these hard to come by at present and even if you do find offers, the interest rates will be higher

- Deposit 25% = 75% LTV (loan to value) interest rates will be competitive but not cheap. This is the most popular option for many investors although some prefer to put as little money down as possible

- Deposit 35% = 65% LTV (loan to value), interest rates will generally be lower

Strategy

If you were to ask which is best to go for, personally I would say for the pension strategy set out in this book, 75% on a first property as this leaves you with some contingency money even if you could afford the 35% deposit for a 65% LTV, but a lot will depend on your future plans, your financial position and your own personal plans. You may have no other choice than to take an 80% LTV mortgage if you can get one initially and it is still better to make a start than sit on the money. Alternatively, you may decide that owning a single buy-to-let property is enough for you because of other investments and so you may want to get the loan paid off as soon as possible. Mortgages are discussed in the next chapter.

Decide on your aim

It is important at the outset to decide on what you are aiming to achieve and therefore decide on the number and type of properties you are aiming to purchase during a specific timescale. You can review this strategy whenever you like and you should certainly do so if there is a change in market conditions or your own personal situation. Otherwise, review every one to two years. The last thing you want to do, though, is wander aimlessly into property investment as you may end up failing and blaming property rather than the lack of preparation.

I can tell you from experience that buying the first property is the most frightening, although possibly the most exciting too. I could give you a random figure and say that you will need £20,000 investment money but it all depends whereabouts you live in the United Kingdom and where you want to invest. It is better, in my opinion, to talk about percentages. One thing is certain though: the less you have initially, the harder it is to get started. But it is not impossible.

If you only have £10,000 to invest you are going to struggle in most parts of the country, but it can still be done. Bear in mind that if you invest all you have, you are going to find it more stressful than someone who is investing a proportion of their savings. For instance, I spoke to a friend a few years ago and she had come into £20,000 and I suggested that she could invest in property; she was unwilling because it was all she had in the world and put it into savings. The money is probably still sitting there with little or no interest or she may have gradually spent it. I haven't asked because it's none of my business. Had she invested at the time, like me, she would be sitting on a 25% capital gain and £3,200 per annum rental gain after tax and expenses which I reinvest. That's a £27,000 capital gain for a £24,000 initial investment so in her case she would have needed to buy a property for a bit less than the one I purchased. Capital growth does not always move this fast as we will discuss later but it gives you an idea of what can be achieved from investing in property.

I have extensively covered looking for property and all of the different types of property in my other book, *Buy to Let: 7 steps to Successful Investing*, if you want to look at the whole procedure in detail, but will cover some of the principles in chapter 5.

Save for the Deposit

I will just mention that if you are a younger person reading this book and have no savings, you need to discipline yourself to get into the savings habit. Each week or month, whenever you get paid put a percentage of your salary into savings. Some people split their money into 10% saving for future, 5% for emergencies (new washing machine, etc.), and then the rest of the salary pays off the bills and provides living expenses. I have to say this again: it depends on what you earn but the minimum you should save is around 10% if you are serious about investing in property.

How Much Is Needed

Let's look at some examples of how much you will need to buy that first rental property. We will take a look at three different examples (cheap, average and expensive) to give you an idea. This is all relative because it depends on your current salary, the type of house you already live in yourself and your own mortgage repayments. Property investment is for everyone with the proviso that you will need to have an annual salary of at least £25,000 as a single investor or joint income of £29,000 to satisfy most lenders and meet their criteria. Some people reading this book will earn just that and others way more. If you earn a much higher salary, you will be able to build up a portfolio much faster (depending on where you spend your money).

You also need to know what type of property you want to buy: a flat, a house, 2 or 3 bedrooms, and so on, and to some extent this will depend on your budget. On the whole I recommend that, for starting out, 2 bedroom houses are ideal because you are less likely to get families (kids cause more damage) and 2 bedrooms provide the opportunity to house share. Flats are ok too but you have to take into account length of lease, maintenance and service charges, and see if these can be absorbed as part of the rent. If you live in a part of the country where flats are popular then that's what to buy. Did I mention you need to research the rental market?

I wouldn't recommend that you buy your first property at auction, although many people do – mainly because it is highly likely that you will pay too much and under-estimate renovation costs (unless you are a builder, of course, in which case I will withdraw that statement). Yes, you did read right, at auction you can pay too much, mainly because people get carried away at auction and can be tempted to overspend. Add to this that the majority of people underestimate the money needed for refurbishment and you can find yourself in a position where the returns are the same, if not less, than buying in the general housing marketplace. Bargains can be found at auction though, and if you do your research and set a ceiling price (and stick to it!), you may come away with a great property to rent out.

Having said that I prefer two bedroom properties – I do own a three bedroom house that is a good rental property, and I have a lovely family living there, but the truth is that house costs me a lot more in maintenance and repairs than the rest of my portfolio. This is for the simple reason that kids are kids and one parent families have enough on their plates without chasing them around the house asking them to be careful about causing minor damage.

Tenants are responsible for making good damages that do not count as wear and tear, and these can be claimed from the deposit at the end of the tenancy. Deposits are protected though, so you will need a good inventory plus photos from the beginning of the tenancy to demonstrate that the damage was not there previously.

You don't have to buy smaller properties, you can buy as big as you like depending where you are purchasing but small properties are easy to manage and easy to let. Some people specialise in Homes of Multiple Occupancy (HMOs) and make a lot of money from them, but they attract stricter legislation and are not for the fainthearted.

Examples

Let's assume then that you are going to buy a 2 bedroom house with an interest only mortgage. We will look at mortgage costs and affordability criteria later in this book.

House 1

Price £55,000
Valuation Fee = £150 (can be higher depending on lender)
Deposit @ 25% = £13,750
Stamp duty @ 3% = £1,650
Solicitors fees plus broker fees = £1,200
Arrangement fee = £1,500 (can be added to loan)

Amount required = £16,750, if you don't pay arrangement fee upfront. If you follow an investment strategy the rest of your portfolio growth will mainly come from this first investment and so you may not need to dip into your savings after your first purchase.

House 2

Price £140,000

Valuation fee = £150

Deposit @ 25% = £35,000

Stamp duty @ 5% = £7,000

Solicitors fees plus broker fees = £1,500

Arrangement fee added to loan

Amount required = £43,650

House 3

Price £295,000

Valuation fee = £150

Deposit @ 25% = £73,750

Stamp duty @ 8% = £23,600

Solicitors fees plus brokers fees = £2,000

Arrangement fee added to loan

Amount required = £99,500

The only difference if you were buying a flat rather than a house would be you need to add the ongoing expenses of ground rent and maintenance fees, and check that the lease is long enough to make the purchase worthwhile.

You can see the obvious from the examples above that the cheaper the purchase price, the less money you need to pay upfront. If you were buying with cash you would still need to find the stamp duty and other fees in addition to the purchase price. The great thing about buying a rental property, be it with cash or a mortgage, is that you are classed as a NTS (nothing to sell) purchaser and this puts you in a stronger negotiating position.

The reason for the stronger position is that like first time buyers you will close a chain and generally complete a lot faster than someone with a property to sell. The advantage you have over first time buyers is that you have proven creditability and are more likely to be in a financially stable position. In spite of the changes to affordability criteria imposed on property investors, you are still more likely to have a loan approved as long (as you have not over borrowed).

How to Get Deposit

We have already seen that in the majority of cases a 25% deposit will be required. So how much do you need? I have shown in the examples that it depends on the purchase price and you need to take into account the additional costs.

I have just carried out an online property portal search and found 2 bedroom properties in the North East priced between £30,000 - £50,000 so the deposit required would be between £7,500 - £12,500, plus the required expenses. This is just to demonstrate that you do not have to have huge amounts of money initially if you were to buy in some parts of the country.

In the local area where I live, the average two bedroom property costs between £140,000 and £155,000 and is rising. Here you would need between £35,000 - £38,750 deposit plus expenses. In South East London you can expect to purchase a 2 bedroom property (usually flats) for in excess of £200,000 meaning a minimum of £50,000 plus expenses required. This is at the lower end of the London market and in the majority of cases you can expect to pay much more. I used to own a 2 bedroom property in a mainly council estate in Reading, Berkshire and this is currently estimated at £224,000 which has a 64% capital gain over 12 years.

I think if you have less than £10,000 you are going to struggle to invest in property but it can still be done and if you have £25,000 you are going to find it much easier. There are many different ways in which property investors go about finding the initial deposit to invest in a first investment property.

Savings

We discussed earlier how important it is to have savings and it might be the accumulation of savings that you use to invest in your first property. You may be in the fortunate position of having a large savings pot. If you are, then this is a good place to start. Whether you buy one or more properties is up to you and the amount that you have to invest.

Partnerships

If you don't have enough money to invest yourself, you could consider going into partnership with someone you trust. This can be a family member, spouse, relative or friend. This is not uncommon and many people have started off this way. There are tax benefits to investing with someone else and of course you are halving your risk.

Inheritance

If you have inherited a sum of money, depending on how close you were to the person who is deceased you may not wish to think about it initially. Once you are ready to think about what to do with the money, it could be used to invest in your first or an additional property.

Equity Release

Some people use capital released from their own home to invest in a first buy-to-let property or kick-start a portfolio. You can do this at any time, once your property has enough equity in it to make it a viable option. Not everyone would want to do this because it goes against the desire to be mortgage free, but if used as part of an investment strategy it can serve you well. As with any strategy, seek financial advice.

Pension Release

We have already discussed this a little in Chapter One, but a good way to make use of your pension pot is to use it to invest in property.

Lump Sum/Windfall

If you win the lottery, cash in an endowment policy or release your pension lump sum, you could use some of the money to kick-start your property portfolio.

Borrow Money

Some people borrow money to get started on the property investment ladder. Vicki Wusche speaks a lot about this in her books. There is no reason not to do this as long as you and the person you are borrowing from are clear on the terms of the loan and I would recommend a legally binding contract. Vicki also talks about using credit cards to invest in property but I am not an advocate of that strategy. You have to do what you are comfortable with.

KEY POINTS

These are the main routes to finding a deposit for your first investment property but they are by no means exhaustive.

Solicitors

Solicitors' fees do vary depending on where you live in the country, although there are many online solicitors/conveyancers who offer competitive prices nationwide. If you live in London or the South East it might be worth considering this route. Remember, though, that you usually get what you pay for, so if you anticipate any problems with the property you are buying it is worth paying the extra to ensure that the service you get picks up any issues, particularly if buying at auction (which I don't recommend) the first time you invest in property, unless you can't afford to do it any other way.

Financial Advisors/mortgage brokers

Financial advisors and brokers charge a flat minimum fee now; the rules for Independent Financial Advisors (IFAs) changed a few years ago which is why their advice is no longer free. Most advisors/brokers will not charge you until you apply for the mortgage through them, although some may charge a small fee for the advice offered if you decide not to go with them (this is unusual). Some IFAs will not charge you if they get a decent commission from the lender, but brokers will usually charge a flat fee either way.

When buying a property do make sure that the advisor/broker you use is familiar with buy-to-let properties so that they can find you the best deal and have the knowledge not to put you through an application that might be rejected.

For a list of independent financial advisors, you can Google the term and there will be lists of reputable IFAs in your area.

Stamp Duty Land Tax (SDLT)

A brief note about SDLT, commonly known as 'Stamp Duty', which was increased for purchasing second properties by the previous chancellor, George Osbourne, as part of what is commonly seen as punitive measures against landlords.

Basically, if you buy a second home or an investment property an additional 3% is added to the Stamp Duty that you would normally pay if you were a first time buyer. These fees are explained clearly on my website http://www.buytoletinfo.com and on a video I produced for my YouTube channel, and you can watch this by clicking on the link below if you are reading this on an eReader. If not you can search for the videos using my name. My YouTube Channel can be found by searching YouTube for Buy to Let Information and also check out the website at http://www.buytoletinfo.com

Properties under £40,000, e.g. £39,999, are still Stamp Duty exempt right across the United Kingdom, so if you live in any part of the UK where you can still find properties under £40,000 or this is where you wish to buy, then you save an extra 3% by not paying Stamp Duty. Take into account that

Stamp Duty is considered a capital expenditure and you will be able to claim all capital expenditure back when you sell an investment property. If you plan never to sell, you need to see it as part of the investment costs that will yield a healthy return in the future.

Valuation Fee

A mortgage valuation is carried out by the lender to ensure that the property is worth the amount you are buying it for and the lender will charge you for this, except for when you are re-mortgaging where it will sometimes be offered free of charge. If you want to, you can pay for more in-depth surveys. A home buyers' survey is more thorough than the valuation and a buildings survey is the most thorough. The latter used to be known as a Full Structural Survey. Home buyers' surveys usually cost around £350 and buildings surveys around £500. Some lenders will charge up to £300 just for a valuation. Prices do vary around the country and are likely to be more expensive in London.

Understanding Compounding Interest

Compounding interest is not that difficult to understand. In its simplest form, if you have savings in a bank account (rather than hidden under the bed) you will earn interest. Most bank interest rates in the present day will not earn you an interest rate above that of inflation, which means that although you are making more money than if your savings were under the bed; your money is not worth that much more because inflation is making things more expensive. You may be able to buy a Bond or invest in a long-term savings account that beats inflation but these are not providing you with any income now. That is good, when you are investing for the future because you are locking money away.

If you were to have invested £1,000 in the stock market over 30 years ago, it should be worth £5,000 today which is a 500% gain. If you had re-invested dividends, therefore compounding, the amount would now be around £14,000 (1,400%) which is compounding the interest or investment in this case. This only happens if the investments made are sound. The same occurs in cash ISAs: if the interest is kept

54

in the account, it makes the overall value of the ISA worth much more than if the interest had been withdrawn. The only caveat with all of this is that you have to keep moving your money in order to attract competitive rates.

Many people remember endowment mortgages taken out over 25 years that didn't meet expectations. One friend had taken out an endowment mortgage costing £38 per month in 1992 which cashed in at £18,000 at term. That's still around a 60% gain on the overall investment but came nowhere near the predicted £32,000 target. Consider, though, that the investment was only £456 per annum. The reason many people do not like dealing with the stock market is the fees that are paid to brokers and other costs incurred are costly, and which even the most financially astute of us do not understand. This is the same for pensions: we have no idea where the money is being invested and no control over the amount we will eventually get. Having said this, a good fund manager should make you some money over time but not as much as with property because of the power of leverage.

Understanding Good Debt versus Bad Debt

There is a world of difference between good debt and bad debt, if you don't already. It is not surprising that for many people, debt has become a way of life and for some, a never-ending vicious cycle. What is even more astonishing is how blasé a whole generation has become with the amount of debt it owns. Part of the reason for this is due to low interest rates. There are extreme cases where people are so desperate they end up going to loan companies charging incomprehensible and obscene rates of interest in my opinion.

It is a long time since the country experienced high interest rates and this has lulled many into a state of complacency. So what exactly is bad debt?

Bad debt

Bad debt is debt is where you owe money on things that take money away from you and do not give you any money back in return.

Examples

- University loans
- Car loans
- Credit cards unless balance paid monthly
- Hire purchase

All of these things take money away from you and although, in some cases they offer pleasurable things in return, they are still classed as bad debt because you will never get any money back. The one exception for some people might be the university education if they end up with a high paid job as a result but this should not be automatically assumed. Many plumbers, electricians & builders will earn more money than some people with university degrees.

Good Debt

Good debt comes from loans invested in an asset

Okay, so what is good debt? Good debt is money borrowed to buy something called an asset. An asset gives you a return on your investment, therefore putting money in the bank. A mortgage on a buy-to-let property is classed as good debt because the mortgage loan is paid by someone else (a tenant) whilst also supplying the landlord with a passive income. The property itself is an asset because not only does it provide an income but because of the historic property cycle, it will yield capital gains in the long term.

A residential home is not an asset because it is where you live and is taking money away from you rather than providing money for you and your family. That said, over time, it can become an asset, and releasing equity out of a home to invest in an asset can be beneficial. Equity release is discussed in more detail in chapter 8.

Example of Good Debt

- Buy-to-let mortgage for a house costing £125,000
- Interest-only payment on a 75% mortgage of £180 per calendar month
- Rent £550 per calendar month

This leaves the landlord with the mortgage paid and £370 per month in the bank minus tax and expenses. In addition to this, by the end of the mortgage term the property will have accrued capital gains. This is good debt.

Example of Bad Debt

Car loan for purchase of a car costing £10,000 with a deposit of £2,000, repaid at 5.4% interest over 5 years = £189.96 per calendar month with a total cost of £11,397.33 whilst the value of the car falls to approximately a third of purchase price. This is bad debt.

Understanding Property Leverage

Leverage is the part of property which I love and, once understood, shows why property makes so much sense as an investment. When you buy an investment property, you will put down a 25% deposit usually, so for a property costing £120,000 you will put down £30,000. If you were to invest that £30,000 in the stock market that would be your total investment because you would not be able to borrow £90,000 on top in order to make more profits! You would also need to pay additional fees to a fund manager who would take a percentage of profits unless you were investing by yourself. Even when investing yourself, the stock broker you buy through has annual charges and buying and selling fees. Buying and selling can cost around £10-£12 per transaction, less if you make regular transactions.

Here are two examples where we look at a growth of 10% for simplicity. Stock market returns vary depending on your investments.

Example 1

Stock Market £30,000 investment, growth of 10% = £3,000 capital gain, remember that through compounding interest and reinvesting dividends your returns will be significantly higher over time. I don't want to be unfair to the stock market because some people make a lot more money than this, and some people make a lot less or even lose money.

Example 2

A property costing £120,000 with an initial investment of £30,000 with a capital gain of 10% = £12,000. The return here is four times that of the stock market growth investing the same amount of money initially. This is because a mortgage is a leveraged product which means that you make profit on the amount the bank has loaned you! If you re-invest your profits you make even more from the same principle of compounding interest.

This is one of the main reasons why investing in property makes sense to most people. In addition to this you have complete control over where you invest your money. For example, if you would want to be an ethical investor, you would make far less money on the stock market due to the lower returns on ethical investments. Even if you are not worried about investing in things like tobacco and guns, you could still make more money through property over time. Note: I say over time because these types of investments need time due to market volatility and the occasional crash that will occur at some stage during a 25-30 year cycle.

If you are convinced that property looks like a good fit for you, let's go on to look at mortgages. Don't forget: if you already have a pension, that is your stock market investment and it is always good to diversify.

Chapter 4

Mortgages

The first thing to say about buy-to-let mortgages is that, as with home mortgages, most lenders will offer an initial discounted rate on their mortgage products. The most commonly discounted period is for two years, but it can be longer.

Buy-to-let mortgages (BTL) have higher interest rates than ordinary home purchase mortgages, so you will need to be aware of that. Brokers and financial advisors are usually able to get the best deals as some lenders will not offer BTL loans to the general public, except via a broker.

Repayment or Interest Only

This book is about buying property for a pension and in this case, where possible, if starting early in life, you will be looking at repayment mortgages. If repayment mortgages are unaffordable, do not exclude interest only mortgages as you can still build up a healthy pension pot with these too.

Many property investors opt for interest only mortgages in order to finance the building of their portfolio and to supplement their income as the monthly payments are lower. Tax benefits also used to be a big draw for interest only mortgages, but these benefits are being removed over the next four years and tax relief will drop on mortgage interest to only 20%. The tax relief from 2020 for an interest only mortgage will not come off your profit until the pre-tax profit has been calculated, meaning some landlords will be in the higher rate tax band.

You may have read a lot about these tax changes in the news and landlords are certainly not happy with the changes. This is because all of the loan interest was counted as expenditure at year end and could be deducted from rental income before tax was deducted which kept profits under control. For higher rate tax payers it therefore kept costs down. Basic rate taxpayers will not be affected by the changes unless they are pushed into the higher tax band.

How this works in Practice

- Year 1 2017-2018 the amount that can be offset against income is 75% and the other 25% will attract 20% tax relief after income is calculated
- Year 2 2018-2019 the amount that can be offset is 50% with 50% attracting 20% tax relief
- Year 3 2019-2020 the amount that can be offset is 25% with 75% attracting 20% tax relief
- Year 4 and onwards 0% can be offset and net income is calculated for tax and then the 100% loan interest attracts 20% tax relief.

If you are just starting out, none of this will matter too much because you won't have known it to be any different and you can work out whether you can afford to invest in property from now. If you are hoping to buy in the next 12 months, though, you will need to factor in these changes. Table 4.1 shows how the changes will affect net income and tax due over the next few years. It is a bit complex to understand for the next three years due to the movement of net profit and when the loan interest becomes deductable.

The amount of tax due for a basic rate taxpayer will remain the same mostly, but if you are near the higher rate tax threshold then you may get pushed into the higher rate tax bracket. The higher rate tax threshold is currently rising, thankfully, which means that you can earn more before paying higher rate. You may end up paying tax at the higher rate before you retire if your earnings are high. If this is likely to happen to you, just be careful that you are still on target for your retirement plan and that, for now, the rental income still covers your mortgage repayments, expenses and additional tax burden. Higher rate tax is only paid on the amount you earn that falls above the threshold set.

	2017-2018	2018-2019	2019-2020	2020 Onwards
Rental Income	7,200	7,200	7,200	7,200
Expenses	1,000	1,000	1,000	1,000
Mortgage Interest	3,480 ~~-870~~ (25%) = 2,610	3,480 ~~-1740~~ (50%) = 1,740	3,480- ~~2610~~ (75%)=870	0
Net Profit (before tax)	3,590	4,460	5,330	6,200
Tax due 20% tax payer	718	892	1,066	1,240
Tax due 40% tax payer	1,436	1,784	2,132	2,480
Tax relief (20%) of loan interest can be claimed back	174	348	522	696
Actual Tax due 20% tax payer	544	544	544	544
Actual Tax 40% tax payer	1,262	1,436	1,588	1,784

Table 4.1 Changes to tax relief on Mortgage Interest up to 2020

You may not be able to afford a repayment mortgage on your Buy-to-let property and may need to opt for an interest only mortgage. This does not mean that you can't pay lump sums off your mortgage; indeed, many lenders encourage the facility and you can do so at any time. Some lenders penalise you for certain repayments during a discounted period, usually over a certain percentage. Make sure that you ask about this when applying for a mortgage through a broker.

You may also want to know that the mortgage you take out is portable. This means that if you sell and buy another property, you can take the mortgage with you. I will explain a little bit more about BTL mortgages in the next part of this chapter.

Interest only

With an interest only mortgage, you borrow a certain amount of money, for example £100,000, but only pay off the interest each month meaning that you still owe the £100,000 at the end of the mortgage term. Although this may sound scary, it is a common way of borrowing to develop a property investment portfolio because the monthly repayments are much lower than with a repayment mortgage, therefore allowing profit to be taken out and used as passive income or to build up for the next property purchase.

As this book is about funding a pension through property, your overall aim should be to own as many properties as you need outright by the time you retire with no mortgage if you want to be debt free when you retire. If, however, you are starting out later in life with only a small amount of capital to invest you can still build a property portfolio using interest only loans. I have done this as it makes financial sense. The lower repayments mean that you will have a higher profit margin each month and capital gains should come into effect by the time you retire.

You may need to sell one or two properties at the end of term to pay off the others in your portfolio or you can extend the mortgage term as some lenders allow BTL borrowing to continue until you're 75. The new life expectancy is likely to be 90; 60 is the new 50 and so on, so don't see this as old. Although, you are still likely to want to retire at a younger age, particularly if you are in a stressful job, this doesn't mean that you have to stop investing in property at the same time. In fact, you could still be expanding your portfolio at that time if you wanted to!

KEY POINTS

- You can usually pay off lump sums anytime during the mortgage term so you could still be mortgage free by the end if you take advantage of this facility while the property market is hot
- Paying out less each month allows you to reinvest and buy more properties in a shorter space of time
- Paying out less each month usually enables you to negotiate your way through a property market crash
- If you do not pay off any lump sums you will owe the total amount borrowed
- Many landlords rely on house price increases to land them a capital gains profit at the end of the term
- Inflation makes the amount you owe at the end of the term of less value than when you took it out (compare your salary from 25 years ago to now or cost of living)
- Mortgages for BTL can be extended up to the age of 75 and this may increase as life expectancy rises

Repayment Mortgages

If you are in a well-paid job, earn a decent salary and can afford the monthly repayments while fitting the lender's affordability criteria, this is the way to go to be mortgage free at pensionable age if that's your aim. You will then be able to live on the maximum profits in retirement because you will have no mortgages on your own property nor on any of your rental properties. Repayment mortgages mean that you are paying off some of the capital each month as well as interest on the outstanding amount.

This option is not always affordable in the buy-to-let arena, particularly when starting out so don't be obsessed by it as interest only mortgages should not frighten you as long as you don't over borrow. It does make sense to go this way if you can afford it, if you are only aiming for a small portfolio to fund your retirement.

KEYPOINTS

- More money to payout each month so less immediate profit

- Paying out more each month may make it difficult to fund the mortgage during a property crash
- You should be able to pay off lump sums to shorten the term of the mortgage or the monthly repayments
- By the time you retire, you are debt free and the rental income is your pension
- You have a steady income for the rest of your life while property prices are still likely to increase. If you need a lump sum you can sell one of your properties (profits liable to Capital Gains Tax)
-

The Best of Both Worlds

As already discussed, it is not always possible to opt for a repayment mortgage but many lenders offer what is commonly known as a 'part & part' mortgage. You won't usually be able to find these on search engines but they are what it says on the tin. Part Interest only, part repayment mortgage. If you are worried about interest only but can't afford repayment this type of mortgage may help you sleep better at night. You decide on the percentage of the part & part by what you can afford. Any good broker or financial advisor should be able to give you figures on a variety of percentages. I have a part & part mortgage on one of my properties.

KEY POINTS

- Part & part mortgages mean part interest only, part repayment
- Percentages can be worked out on what you can afford to pay
- If you borrow £100,000 with 40% repayment and 60% interest only, you will owe £60,000 at the end of the term.
- You can still pay lump sums off the interest only part of the mortgage
- The monthly repayment is more than an interest only mortgage but lower than a repayment
- It may provide a psychological boost to know that you are paying off a percentage of the property
- You should be able to negotiate comfortably through a property crash as long as you have not over borrowed

Affordability Criteria 2017

In a drive to ensure that buy-to-let investors will be able to afford future interest rate rises, lenders have imposed a higher level of affordability criteria for borrowing on investment properties. The calculation is now based around an increase in the stress test for mortgage interest rates and an increase in the percentage of the rental coverage ratio on mortgage costs.

Some lenders require rental income to cover 140% of monthly mortgage costs and many will be moving to 145%; some still use 125% but these will become few and far between. The new rules do not currently apply to five-year fixed rate mortgages.

The stress test mortgage interest rate is 5.5% (some brokers can find lower stress testing). This does not mean that the interest rate you are paying will be 5.5% - it should be lower than this but the lender will calculate affordability as if you were paying this amount. Some lenders have introduced a stress test of 5.99%, and it will be up to your broker or IFA to shop around.

Examples:

These examples show raw figures and in many cases the actual amounts will be lower than these so please check with a broker, IFA or lender.

Mortgage at stress test rate of 5.5% for a mortgage taken out over 25 years would be assessed at:

Interest only

Borrow £100,000
Calculation at 5.5% = £458 per month
Rent @ 140% of £458 = £641.20

In this example, the monthly mortgage payments calculated at 5.5% means that your rental income for the property would need to be £642 which is achievable on a property requiring a £100,000 mortgage. If you could find a broker who can get a stress test of 4.99%, the monthly rent could be reduced to £583 which may be more realistic for property at this price. Just to reiterate: you won't actually be paying out £458 per month but that is how the stress testing will work out.

Landlords are not happy about these changes because they are going to have to increase rents. Watch this space.

Repayment

Borrow £100,000
Stress test 5.5% = £614 per month
Rent @ 140% = £859.60

In this example, it would make it almost impossible to take out a repayment mortgage as the chances of achieving that kind of rent on a property at this end of the market is nigh on impossible.

Part & part would be lower than repayment but higher than interest only and might be the way to go if you do want to go for repayments.

Remember your loan repayments will be less at present as mortgage interest rates for BTL are currently less than 4%. The stress test is applied to test whether you can afford your repayments if (or when) interest rates rise.

When you calculate the figures, you will see what sort of mortgage you will be able to afford as well as the property price you can pay.

Visit the website https://www.buytoletinfo.com for brokers and insurers, and feel free to contact me via that website for a referral to the broker that I use. At present their stress test amount is 4.99%, but this could change if the Bank of England imposes further restrictions on lenders.

Workarounds

There are a few ways to reduce the burden of the costs and rent requirements of the new affordability criteria.

Fixed (5 years)

At present the criteria is not imposed on mortgages that are fixed for 5 years and so if you definitely want to go for a repayment mortgage while charging a realistic rent for the property, this is worth considering.

Incorporating

Some professional landlords may build a property portfolio by starting a limited company where the restrictions on borrowing are more affordable, but this is unlikely to be a route that most people investing for a pension are going to want to take. For this reason, I will not be discussing corporations in this book but I have recorded a video on the subject which you will find a link to on the website mentioned above.

More Money Down

By putting more money down, you will be borrowing less and therefore will be more likely to fit into any affordability criteria imposed by lenders. For instance, by putting an extra £10,000 into the property above you would be seeking a £90,000 mortgage which would reduce a repayment mortgage to £553 (rent needed £775) under the stress test and an interest only to £412 (rent needed £577) and somewhere in-between for a part and part mortgage.

Buy Higher Yielding Properties

By buying at the lower end of the market and in cheaper areas, you will be able to meet the new criteria as your overall yield will be much higher. Properties at the more expensive end of the market tend to offer lower yields and are therefore less likely to meet the added tests. Buying property below £100,000 will give you higher yields although capital growth may not be as much, but for a pension it is mainly rental income you are after for the future.

Buy Cash

If you can afford to buy property for cash, this might be the way to go as mortgage rules and regulations will not apply to you. The alternative is to buy a few properties with more money down as mentioned above.

Flip Properties to Build Income

By flipping properties you will be able to grow your income faster. Flipping is discussed in the chapter relating to building your portfolio.

KEY POINTS

- Affordability criteria is stricter
- Do your sums before applying for a BTL mortgage
- Remember you will be paying less than the figures above show, these only demonstrate stress testing
- Check rental prices in the area before buying
- Check that your strategy is achievable within the new rules
- Consider the workarounds that will enable you to build up a portfolio in the current market

Chapter 5

Research

Where to Buy

Deciding where to buy is probably going to be the most important decision you make because this will set the tone of your portfolio for the future. To some extent this is going to be dependent on what you can afford, the type of property you opt to buy and what you are comfortable with but there are some general tips.

Close to home

If you can afford to buy in an area with which you are familiar, this is a good idea, as you are less likely to come across surprises. You will be familiar with the housing, transport, good or less good streets, and saleability for the future. You will want to buy in an area that is easily accessible if you are going to manage the property yourself, but even if you intend to use a letting agent it makes sense to buy locally if you can for viewings, repairs, etc.

Even when buying close to home it should form part of your research to delve into an area through a postcode search. Check out the postcode of the street and/or area you are looking at. You can then get all sorts of demographic information just by entering an area or street postcode into the search box at <u>neighbourhood statistics</u> at <u>http://www.neighbourhood.statistics.gov.uk/dissemination</u>.

The neighbourhood statistics website provides freely available census information and will provide information on the area including:

- Percentage of carers
- Types of work occupations
- General health of the population
- Age bands, number of males, females
- How it relates to other parts of the country in terms of crime, income, employment, education, deprivation

You can get some really interesting information from this which might save you a lot of wasted time. You can then compare it to other streets a few miles away. Beware not to be too fussy though because you want to rent in an area that's popular with tenants and that will include some of the areas where there are fewer professionals. What the search will do, though, is help you focus your search on the type of tenant you would be looking for (e.g. If you decide to rent to people on benefits you can look at the areas where there are more people out of work, similarly if you are looking for employed professionals you can hone in on those).

Another site you could use prior to deciding where to buy is one that provides you with information on the postcode that gives a risk rating for subsidence, flooding, coal mining, radon, previous landfill, pollution, etc. The site is *www.homecheck.co.uk*. It only provides information for the street postcode, not the individual property, but it is useful to check. Take into consideration that even in a subsidence risk area, the property you are interested in may never suffer from subsidence, but it helps you to know what to look out for. It will also help inform what type of survey you may wish to have undertaken.

Research the area where you would like to buy property, looking at prices now and over the past ten years. This is easily done via a few websites. Rightmove, Zoopla, Mouseprice and Nethouseprices are search engines that will give you sold prices as well as estimated current values. Also, look at actual and potential rents in the area for the type of property you would like to invest in. Again, the most common property portals are Rightmove and Zoopla, but you can also look in the local papers and ask local estate agents.

There will most likely be areas that you are unfamiliar with even in your own town or city. It may be worth considering these if they are more affordable before buying in different parts of the country. You can use the tools mentioned above to study demographics and environmental risks.

Wherever you buy, speak to the local planning officers to find out if there are any plans for development in the area. Development can be a two-edged sword. Good if it is going to bring money, jobs and new shops into the area. Bad if the area is going to be overdeveloped with too much rental competition.

Out of area

If you buy out of area for price reasons, do your homework. Try to choose an area that is accessible unless you are going to be completely hands off. Some people invest in areas that they would visit fairly regularly anyway, such as places where they have friends or family or areas where they have lived previously. If you buy in a place where you know people, you will already have some sort of feel for the area and your research will be a lot easier.

If you decide on a place that you are not familiar with because you have discovered that house prices are much lower and the demographics are right, visit the area at different times of day. Before visiting, though, make sure you have researched the area on the internet and narrowed it down to a particular location. You will tire very quickly if you take on the whole of Nottingham in a day! Try to visit in the week and over a weekend. Visit local estate agents, check current and sold prices on search engines. You can learn a great deal about an area on the internet, but walking around and imagining a tenant or tenants living there will focus the mind. Obviously, as an investor, you do not want to become overly attached to the properties you are buying (although I am), but you want to provide homes that will give you and the tenant as little trouble as possible.

It is even more likely you will be using a letting agent if you buy out of area so research these at the same time as you research the area. If you want an idea of where to start looking take advantage of the bonus offered at the beginning of this book. Subscribe to my YouTube channel called buytoletinfo.com as I regularly post videos with helpful advice.

Rentable area

People like to rent where there are good transport links. They need access to shops, schools, leisure facilities, universities, jobs, etc. It would be unwise to invest in property in the middle of nowhere unless you plan to get into holiday letting. You would be wise to look up whether there any regeneration plans for the area you are going to invest in. If these plans are not common knowledge, this is even better. It can be a great way to make money as when an area undergoes regeneration, house prices generally go up. For instance, there are parts of the East and West Midlands of England where the HS2 rail link will be passing through in the future. Property prices in and around these areas are relatively cheap at present but they are likely to spike in the future (except if you live in a lovely village where the link is going to pass close by). Although some plans may be very long term and it may be a bit of a risk because building plans can be cancelled, if you are in it for the long haul, you will eventually benefit either way.

Buy near to the tenant market you are targeting, so if you are aiming to rent to students make sure that the property is in an area that is popular with students and that the university is accessible. If you are happy to buy property to let to tenants on benefits you may not need all of the jobs links that other areas have, but generally the house prices in such areas will be more stagnant and see slower growth. Housing benefits also are capped at an upper limit so you may be at risk of tenants defaulting on rent if you set it higher. Having said all this, there is a landlord and a tenant for every type of property, which is why buy-to-let investment is so interesting. You just need to find your own niche.

At the end of the day you need to buy a property that will be easily let and generate a good income, all while minimising void periods. Some of the best rental areas might not be where you would choose to live yourself, but you could chat to people in the area and ask what it is like to live there. You will find people will live anywhere where there are good transport links and where they feel safe.

Check Whether Licensing Has Been Introduced

A relatively new addition to rental bureaucracy has been introduced in the United Kingdom for landlords are registration and/or licensing. The registration of landlords makes sense in many ways so that landlords can be tracked down if there are issues with a property. Licensing is a bit more controversial and a lot more expensive and is therefore being implemented more sporadically, except in Wales.

Landlord Licensing Schemes England

In parts of England selective licensing schemes have been introduced by some local authorities where they have introduced landlord licenses for all properties, not just for HMOs.

Licenses have varying costs but can be anywhere between £200 and £1,000 where they apply, but the penalties for not having a license are punitive at around £20,000. Such schemes were put in place to weed out rogue landlords and antisocial behaviour, but they are costly to landlords where they apply. Contact your local council to find out if the scheme is in place. Before buying property please do check whether the scheme applies and whether it is cost effective to buy property in that area. There are many councils that have introduced the schemes and many others being added each year. Nottingham council is planning to introduce a licensing scheme that will cost landlords £600 per property. Go to my blog to find a link to some of the areas that have schemes at http://www.blog.www.buytoletinfo.com but also ask your council.

Renting in Scotland

All HMOs have to be licensed in Scotland, not just those with three or more floors and/or five or more tenants. Landlords in Scotland have to be registered (but not all licensed) although there are some exemptions, one being if let to family only. The cost of registration is £55 to each local authority that you own houses in. There may be discounts for multiple councils but you will need to enquire. In addition to this you need to pay £11 for each property registered.

Renting in Wales

Rent Smart Wales stems from the Housing Wales Act 2014 and is being managed by Cardiff City Council but applies to the whole of Wales. Initially it was voluntary but now it is compulsory.

As of 23 November 2016, all landlords are required to be registered under the Rent Smart Wales regulations. It is a criminal offence not to be registered. This applies to everyone letting a property in Wales. The cost to register is £33.50 online at the time of writing, although paper applications cost around £80. The landlord only needs to register once, not for every property owned.

Landlords who intend to manage their own properties will also need to complete approved training and apply for a license. There is a cost for approved training courses and these are available from various sources. At present the Welsh Government charges £100. Online courses are cheaper at around £30. Keep an eye on prices as they may change over time. The cost of the license for an individual landlord is at present £144 and the license is valid for five years. If you do not intend to manage any properties you still need to register but do not need a license.

If you intend to manage your own and somebody else's property you need to register, undertake training and pay for an agent license if the number of properties exceeds twenty. Agents also need to be trained and licensed in order to manage property. An agent's license is much more expensive and if you manage more than twenty properties belonging to other people you will be classed as an agent. As a licensed landlord you will be obliged to abide by the Rent Smart Wales Code of Practice which is available on their website.

Renting in Northern Ireland

All landlords in Northern Ireland have to register at a cost of £70 one off fee. There is no licensing yet in NI, but there have been calls to introduce a licensing scheme so this may well change in the near future.

Whilst this legislation does not apply to the whole of England as yet, more and more councils are introducing selective licensing. Scotland and Northern Ireland operate registration schemes only at present, with licenses applying to all HMO properties. The legislation aims to weed out rogue landlords but it comes at a cost to all landlords and governments may introduce legislation for financial as well as ethical gains. Some may be put off from going too far due to the costs of administrating these schemes.

KEY POINTS

- Where possible buy close to home
- Research the area through postcode search
- Visit the area if buying further away
- Check property prices & rental incomes before deciding
- Find out if you need a license

Chapter 6

My 10 Steps to Buying Property

Having gone through this process on a number of occasions now there is a checklist I go through which you can find at the back of this book.

I break this checklist down into 10 steps to buying a property. This seems like a lot of items to tick off, but keep in mind that many of them are small with little work required. We will look at each step in detail and break down what is involved so that there is a clear understanding of the process. Some of the things you will be doing together but for simplicity I have broken it down into really simple bite-sized chunks.

Step 1 Price

This may seem obvious but it is important to know exactly how much money you can afford to put down on a property before you start looking. This will save you lots of wasted time looking at properties that are over your budget. Other calculations need to be taken into account, such as cost of surveys, solicitor's fees, loan application fees, broker fees and mortgage agreement fees. Agreement fees tend to be in excess of £1,000 on buy-to-let properties and many investors, myself included, add these to the loan most of the time because cash flow is important and having an extra one to two thousand pounds to spend on the house or on unforeseen problems is better than being stretched too far.

Add in contingency money if you are thinking of buying property needing refurbishment or updating.

Step 2 What Type of Property?

Having decided on how much you can spend you need to know what you are looking for. It is a good idea to know whether you are happy to look at any kind of property or have a particular type in mind. Put simply, do you want to buy a house or a flat or maisonette? The latter two would be leasehold properties and would therefore incur additional charges that would need to be taken into account, such as ground rent and service charges. Service charges on some modern builds can be monsters, so make sure that you are aware of them before you buy.

I haven't said a lot about Houses of Multiple Occupancy (HMOs), basically houses split into shared accommodation or bedsits, as I am assuming that if you are buying for a pension, you may not want the headache of managing these properties that tend to have a whole load of extra legislation attached, although they are very profitable. If you are interested in these I will discuss briefly the legislation later in the book.

I have bought houses for my portfolio. I have looked at flats on a number of occasions to get a feel for the market, but have found that, where I buy, houses are more profitable. In some areas, rental stock will be mainly flats and it would be sensible to buy what rents if you live in such an area. Flats tend to be very popular in town centres and can be let at a premium. I would definitely buy in a town centre or near a great bus route, university or hospital if I were going to buy a flat.

Step 3 Number of bedrooms

This will, in part, be down to your finances but I lean towards 2 bedrooms for the reasons I mentioned earlier. Sometimes, though, a 3 bedroom property will come up that cannot be ignored and that is why I own one. Although it is great to have an idea what you would like and stick to it first time round, you will become more flexible with more experience without wasting valuable time. One bedroom properties are ok and rent well in many areas, but they are more likely to be higher turnover as people develop relationships and decide to go bigger. One bedroom properties tend to be flats or maisonettes, although there are many one bedroom houses plonked on the end of a row of houses on newer estates. I guess the builders wanted to use up every space! Personally,

I have never considered buying more than 3 bedroom properties – not quite true, I did look at a 7 bedroom HMO once that was selling really cheap at auction. I decided it wasn't my area or expertise or interest and left it at that but some investors make a fortune out of HMOs. Some landlords turn a two bedroom house into a three bedroom HMO because of the obvious attraction of the extra rent. Small HMOs in England do not have to be licensed, although some extra rules apply. It is certainly worth considering if you intend to buy is an area near to a hospital or a university.

We discussed earlier the problem of yield with more expensive properties, so you will need to take this into account, particularly if your budget is tight and you need a mortgage. If a two bedroom property will not give you enough yield you could look at using one of the downstairs rooms to create an HMO if three bedroom properties are out of reach.

Step 4 How to Buy

Search Engines/Estate Agents

This may seem obvious but there are different ways to purchase an investment property. The time-honoured tradition of buying through an Estate Agent is still used in the majority of cases, although local estate agents may become a thing of the past in the not too distant future as more competition develops online. There is a whole new technology-savvy generation who are happy to sell through online agents but we are talking about buying. If you want to buy traditionally – by that, I mean using a local agent and/or and online property portal to do your searching - it is a simple and straightforward process. It is always worth building up a good relationship with local estate agents because they will give you a heads up when a good investment property comes to market. I had such a tip just last month for an absolute bargain house. It's nothing underhand but getting in early when the market is hot is never a bad thing.

Property portal websites are invaluable in terms of the amount of information that can be gleaned from them, including sold prices, area maps, rental values and loads of other useful nuggets of information to help you before you step foot inside the door of a property.

Auction

Buying at auction is a whole different ballgame and it is important to know the rules before going down this route. Firstly, you need to know that at the fall of the hammer, you exchange contracts and have four weeks to complete usually and you will be charged interest for any delays. Secondly, properties are sold at auction for a reason – it is your job to find out what that reason is it is not the job of the auctioneer to tell you although good auctioneers will list using terms such as:

'In need of modernisation'
'In need of refurbishment'

They will not tell you that there is subsidence or that the roof is falling down, nor will they tell you that the lease has only 25 years left on it and so you do need to read through the details, view the property and read the legal pack. Some houses sold at auction are repossessions or deceased estates, and these can often be super purchases so don't let me put you off. Buying at auction is really the subject of a book in itself, although I have included quite a lot of detail in my other book, *Buy to Let: 7 Steps to Successful Investing*, if you are interested. I would recommend that you do watch programmes such as 'Homes Under the Hammer' to get a feel for the auction buying process but consider that the problems with the houses look a lot worse when you walk through the door of a real one. Some, though, are real steals and you may find one. If you are a self-employed tradesperson or builder then buying a property in need of work will be a lot easier for you. I have a team of trades people who I work with and would not have any qualms about buying the right property at auction. If you do go this route, make sure you overestimate your refurbishment costs by 10-20% because most people under-estimate.

Leafleting

A technique some investors use is that of leaflet dropping. If you are ready to roll and have a rough estimate of the house values in your area or are a cash buyer this can be a great way to buy below market value. No investor looking to buy this way is wanting to pay the market value. Sometimes a leaflet will drop through the door of someone wanting to sell quickly or who has been thinking about moving but not gotten around to doing anything about it. Your leaflet could be the nudge they have been waiting for.

Sourcing Property

Some people use others to source and buy properties for them and then hand over the management either to them or to an agent. This will incur costs, but if you are cash rich and time poor then this is a viable option. You can find many property sourcers through online searches or landlord websites. You will also find that people who write books like this either teach property investment courses or source properties for people, so check out some of the other property books out there.

Book a Consultation

If you are wondering whether it is something I would do, the answer is yes but I would only source property in the East

Midlands. Feel free to contact me via the website at http:www.buytoletinfo.com if this would be something you would like to discuss. I also offer skype or facetime consultations if you would like to talk through a strategy so feel free to contact me.

Beware of rogues and if you do find an online company, check out their reviews. Also consider trying to pose as a customer before using them to see if you would be comfortable with the way they do business. If you can, do a viewing as a potential customer and check out their professionalism and legitimacy.

There are property investment companies who get involved with large city centre new builds that will source luxury off-plan apartments for you and offer percentage yields. Again, many of these are legitimate businesses but check the small print and do some research yourself to see if the numbers add up before investing.

Step 5 Where to Buy

Initially, most people will consider buying close to home as this will be an area that is known to them. However, some people will not want to buy on their own patch because they will want to be distanced from the investments and resist the temptation to drive down the street to see what is going on with the property. For some, where you buy will depend on money – in fact for most of us, this is the bottom line.

If you are determined to buy close to home but don't quite have enough money you could save up until you do with increased determination. For most people reading this book, you are looking to invest in property for a pension (otherwise you may have picked up the wrong book) and it would be better for you if you stay emotionally detached from the property you are buying. If you were investing in the stock market you would definitely not be attending all the shareholder meetings and it is unlikely you would be buying shares in a company down the road. See it as an investment for the future and not as something that you want to engage with in an emotional way, unless you want to manage the properties yourself and even then you need a certain amount of detachment.

For simplicity's sake, though, you know the property prices in your own area and it would be much easier for you to view such properties while also developing a good relationship with a few local estate agents. This makes good financial sense and will save you a lot of time traipsing up and down motorways viewing properties out of area.

If you do venture out of area, it is worth considering places that you are familiar with, perhaps where you have lived previously, or where friends or relatives live. The reasons for this are fairly obvious: you will either have some knowledge of the area or your friends/family will have knowledge of an area. If there are no affordable areas falling into this category, and even if there are, it is time to do the additional research and narrow the area down.

This research would include looking at rentable and affordable areas depending on your price range and the type of tenant you are looking for. Eventually you will narrow it down to an area within a town or city that you can start searching for properties in. Once you have narrowed it down try not to deviate or you will make the search time much longer as you will have to do the research over again.

Now is the exciting part. You can start searching the property portals online and either visit/email or call estate agents in the area, depending on distance. There is a whole chapter in my book, *Buy to Let: 7 Steps to Successful Investing*, dedicated to looking for property with a lot more detail, including the things you need to consider such as finding property fit for market. This means that your property needs to be suitable for the tenant/s you are looking to rent to. Things to be taken into consideration are bus routes, employment, schools, hospitals, universities, etc.

You will soon discover the ceiling price range for the type of property you are looking for, and ideally you will want to buy well below this and, if possible, below market value. Once you have decided on the amount of money you have to spend you can start looking. Some investors look at properties priced below their ceiling and some will look at properties +/- £10,000 depending on their negotiating skills. It really is up to you what you look at, but don't be tempted to overspend. Cash flow is important to any business and this is true for investing in property too. We will look at cash flow later in this book.

Market Value

This is a tricky one, because a property is worth what a person is willing to pay for it. There is, however, usually a ceiling price which is where houses in pristine condition will sit. There will also be a lower end price for houses that are either not as popular for some reason or that are in need of some decorative work. In stock market terms this is known as support and resistance with the higher price being resistance and the lower price being the support. You will know from the area where you currently live that there are some streets or smaller areas that are cheaper for some reason and this will be true of every area. An outsider might wonder why the price differs, and can end up paying too much. It is always important to do research.

If a property is in need of major refurbishment, it should be listed well below market value but this is not always the case. Some agents or owners feel that if they reduce the price by the estimated cost of refurbishment, this is enough but they are not taking into account your time or indeed your loss of income while a property is being refurbished so the price you would offer needs to take these additional factors into consideration. As an investor, you really do not want to be paying too much for a property. That doesn't mean you can't buy for a fair price – remember this is a pension you are aiming for; you are not looking to flip a property, as most property traders do.

When viewing the properties online take a look at which postcodes are priced higher and which are lower. Look at the houses and the decor. Most search engines default to highest price first which is useful, but you can also switch the filter to show the lowest price first so that you can work upwards and see what the differences are. Other filters you can add in are 'include sold subject to contract' which is useful because, although it will not tell you what the offer price is, it will give you the start price and you can work out what you would be willing to pay or offer for those properties. Once you have built up a rapport with an agent you can ask whether properties are going for at or around asking price and they might be honest with you. If you know that properties are selling at asking price in an area, you might need to switch if you can't afford to buy at this price or you can make your offer at a certain level below this and eventually someone who wants a quick sale will accept your offer. Don't become emotionally attached and be happy to walk away. There will always be another property around the corner (perhaps literally).

Once you have done your search and have a list of properties, create a shortlist of the number you plan to view. This number may depend on whether you are buying out of area. If you are, you will want to look at a bunch of properties over a single weekend or weekday, whenever you have time. If you can't view one particular property then leave that one unless you don't find anything else to put an offer on. It might be worth doing a few practice runs before you are serious about buying so that you get a feel for what the property market is doing in an area and what properties are available.

Step 6 Viewing & Offers

If you are buying in an area where friends or family live, you could ask them to view and screen for you as long as they are clear on your criteria. When you have your shortlist, go through it so that you know as much as you can prior to viewing. Write down any things that stand out or questions that aren't addressed in the brochure. Make sure that you take a notebook with you, particularly if you are viewing out of area, as its easy for all of the properties to merge into one.

Prior to viewing, keep an eye on how quickly property is moving: if one property has been on the market for a long time while others sell within a few weeks of listing, there will be a reason for this. Having said that, you, as an investor, might be able to live with that reason if it is a matter of refurbishment and the seller will be much more likely to negotiate. Some of the reasons a property might stay on the market for longer:

- In need of refurbishment
- Cluttered – it is amazing how many people can't see a bargain behind the clutter which is very good for investors
- In need of moderate refurbishment, e.g. new bathroom or kitchen
- No gas/central heating. It can cost between £2,000 - £4,000 to have gas central heating put into a property where there is already a gas supply and more if there is no gas supply

- In need of complete renovation – the price should reflect this (property might be sold at auction)
- Seller has unrealistic expectations and/or is intransigent
- Non-standard construction
- No kerb appeal
- In a less popular area
- Short lease on a flat or maisonette

The list is not exhaustive and there can be many more reasons. With experience, you will learn to spot immediately what the issue is or an agent may be able to give you some information.

Properties that are likely to sell quickly and where sellers may be more open to negotiation:

- Low price for quick sale
- Relationship breakup
- Owner needs to move away for work, etc.
- Seller in financial difficulty, e.g. lost job
- Seller has moved into a care home
- Deceased estate

- Seller has found dream home and doesn't want to lose it
- Landlord disposing of properties

It seems a bit ruthless when you look at some of these in black and white, but the reality is that these sellers are more likely to accept low offers from an investor due to their circumstances. You may or may not be aware of any of these circumstances, but any one of these might be a reason for a lower offer being accepted. On the flip-side there are sellers who are in no rush to sell and will hold out for the very last penny, even down to the last £500. As an investor, walk away from the latter because you are not buying a dream home and you do not want to waste your time.

After the viewing, make a list of your preferred properties and the price you are willing to offer. List them in order of preference that could be based on price, rentability or likelihood of seller accepting the offer.

Shortlist for Offers

Hopefully, following viewings you have developed a shortlist of properties that you are happy to put an offer on. Decide on the maximum amount you are willing to offer and offer below that price. A basic rule of thumb is that the higher the asking price the more you will want to take off, depending on location. If you are in a slow moving market, you would offer even less. You can buy properties at full asking price where you know that the asking price is reasonable or priced low for a quick sale and that the property is likely to increase in value in a very short space of time.

Properties bought three years ago have undergone a 25% and one has a 30% capital gain in the area where I buy. In many ways, this is irrelevant because the properties are not for sale but it is good to know that the investments made are increasing in value. Of course, this could change and reverse but it would still not matter as long as the mortgages are being paid and the income is higher than the expenses.

If your offer is accepted first time, great, you have spent less than you were willing to (nice when this happens). If not, you can put in your next offer £1,000 at a time at the lower end of the market, higher if you are buying at the upper end, until you reach your final offer price. If it is still not accepted then it is probably time to move on to property number two or start viewing again if there is not a suitable property number two or if it has sold.

Before making the offer, it is worth doing a pros and cons list. List all the things that you think are good about the property and all the things that you think are going to cost you money or slow you down in any way when it comes to completion. If the property does need refurbishment, try to calculate how much that is going to cost and take that into consideration before making an offer. You will also need to have a rental estimate before you make an offer so do some research on a property portal site or go into a few estate agents. If you know the area, you will already have an idea.

If you're not going to use an agent to manage your property, you can go in as a mystery shopper and ask them what sort of prices properties are letting for at the type you are looking at. I find agents sometimes underestimate when you ask as a landlord because they want to let the property quickly and make the most money, so I would usually ask for slightly higher, you can always go down but you can't go up initially.

Also, check the property portals to see what properties are renting for in the category you are buying.

Once you have a rental estimate you need to think about whether the property price is negotiable. Do you think the seller is going to negotiate? If not, don't worry you can walk away. It is always worth making an offer because, as I said previously, if it is rejected you move onto the next property.

Another thing you want to consider in terms of refurbishment is how much is going to be needed and how much this is going to cost you. When estimating refurbishment costs add an extra few hundred – thousand pounds (depending on the amount required) as there are always unforeseen issues that crop up after you have bought the property. Consider the sellers position: if you are in a hurry you want to know if the seller has found a property to move to. You will be closing a chain, which is your major bargaining chip, and this is why sellers will accept lower offers from investors because they are closing a chain which makes things easier for the whole chain.

Step 7 Mortgage Agreement in Principle/Cash Buy

Once you are serious about viewing to purchase, it is worth making sure that you have an agreement in principle in place as some agents won't even put an offer to the seller without one. You may need to do this in a different order and have one ready prior to viewings. Once you have a broker or IFA that you know, this can be sorted in an hour so I tend to do it once I have decided on an offer. Also, if I am using an agent that knows me they know that I will be able to sort this out very quickly and will put the offer to the seller.

An Agreement in Principle is where the lender has agreed to finance your mortgage for the top amount you can afford or to your asking price if an offer has been accepted. You don't have to spend the top amount but you can't offer over that amount. You don't have to go with the lender who has provided the agreement when you do have an offer accepted. Many brokers will not charge you for the Agreement in Principle; they will only charge you at mortgage application. Be prepared to spend at least an hour getting this agreement as you will have to provide the majority of the information that would be required if you were applying for a mortgage. If you are new to this it can take up to two hours. Once you are known to a broker, it is much simpler as they will have all of your details on file.

Although the affordability criteria is more stringent now for BTL mortgages, it is still easier than applying for your first home mortgage. Lenders are a bit more wary when you buy your first investment property, but once you have bought and held one property for over twelve months you are classed as an experienced landlord.

Cash Buyer

The world is your oyster, you are in a strong purchasing position and you do not need to jump through the hoops required to obtain a mortgage. The only thing you need to ask yourself in relation to purchasing for a pension is could you use your cash to buy all the properties in a short space of time using your cash as deposits and mortgage as leverage. This makes much more sense in a way for pension security because you are buying years in advance and if you don't need the income from the properties now, you can buy the properties, set them up and more or less forget about them until you are ready to retire.

If you are a bit older and drawing near to retirement, and if you are happy with the income that a cash purchase can provide, this too could be the right thing for you. This is particularly true if you are debt averse, but always factor in the power of leverage as mentioned previously in relation to investment.

Step 8 Buying Process: Relax

Once you've had your offer accepted it is advisable to leave the solicitors, lender and agent to do their work unless you think they are going too slowly, in which case give them a nudge. Try not to stress about it. The whole idea is that you are investing for the future and you want it all to be as stress free as possible. A good agent will chase up lenders and solicitors to keep the whole process moving along. Some lenders are slower than others, particularly if it is your first buy-to-let purchase because they want to make sure that you can afford it and they will do all their affordability tests. Be prepared to give them at least three months' worth of

117

bank statements and payslips. If you are self employed they are likely to request 6-12 months' worth of accounts. If you are working there is not usually a problem getting a buy-to-let mortgage because you are likely to meet their lending criteria.

Insurance

You will need to take out landlord's buildings insurance for the property and also contents if you intend to let a partially or fully furnished property. The costs depend on the type of tenants you are taking on and the cost of rebuilding. There are fairly hefty buildings insurance excesses so make sure that you are happy with these. The cheapest buildings insurance will be if you let to working people, the most expensive is likely to be for HMOs. Properties of non-standard construction may need specialist insurers. You shouldn't need to go with the lenders recommended insurer generally. Please see my website at www.buytoletinfo.com for competitive insurers.

If the property is empty, the insurance is different and more costly. The property has to be insured from exchange of contracts if you are taking out a mortgage.

Step 9 Letting Property

Once you are getting near to exchange of contracts it is worth putting out feelers for tenants. You may have people already lined up or you may not. As you are investing for the future it is highly likely that you will be putting your property with a letting agent. Research agents' costs and then get in early. Explain that you are in the process of purchasing a property to rent out, that you are expecting to exchange contracts on such-and-such a date, and that you want to get the property on the market as soon as possible.

Once you have a completion date you can let them know and they can start advertising once you have exchanged contracts. There is no reason why they can't use the description that was used to sell the house and they will use the Energy Performance Certificate (EPC) from the sale. They obviously won't advertise prior to exchange of contracts in case the sale falls through. Ideally, if there is no refurbishment required or no major refurbishment, you will want viewings to be taking place as near to completion date as possible. The sooner people are viewing, the sooner you will let the property, the sooner you can have rent coming in covering your outgoings.

Negotiate Letting Fees

Many letting agents charge 12% of rental income plus VAT but this is negotiable. I have never paid higher than 10%. Use the fact that you will be adding to your portfolio as a negotiating tool. Once you accept the fees it is difficult to change them and you always need to get the best deal possible. Shop around for agents, but make sure you find one that is well respected among landlords and in the local area.

The last thing you want to be doing is running around after an agent who is not doing their job properly. Once the property is let you can then get on with your life and forget about the property.

What to Expect from an Agent

Once you have agreed the tenancy, and if you are letting the agent fully manage, leave it alone, let them do their job. If they don't do their job, by all means chase them up and let them know the standard of service you require.

You need an agent that you can trust and leave the property with, otherwise why pay them? The only time you will then need to have any dealings with them is when they contact you to let you know of a maintenance request or that a tenant has given notice.

The agent will arrange the annual gas safety certificate for you and you can let them know if you would like a boiler service to be carried out at the same time each year. They should let you know of any changes in legislation. They should inspect the property three monthly to check that the tenants are treating the property in the right way and let you know of any issues. They will take the deposit from the tenant and lodge it with the appropriate deposit protection scheme to conform with the required government legislation.

They will also arrange for renewal of contracts. Some agents will charge every time they renew a contract, others will only charge again if there is a change of tenancy. The ideal position you want to be in is that of buying a property, seeing it let and then moving on with your life and the next property.

121

There are additional fees that agents can charge for so do check what is included in the management service you are paying for. Chapter 13 looks at letting agents in more detail.

Managing Property Yourself

As I have said before, in the majority of cases, people reading this book will be handing their property over to be managed by a lettings agent, particularly if you continue to work full time. If you are in a position where you are semi-retired, made redundant or want to reduce your working hours you might want to manage the property yourself.

Managing property yourself will be discussed later in this book. Tenancy management does change a lot so you will need to work out how you intend to keep up to date with changes. Landlord forums are a great place to do this.

Step 10 Rinse & Repeat

This is the easy bit if you are not managing the property yourself; you just leave it with the agents and forget about it. You now carry on with your life until you are ready to buy the next one and then you start over again, but this time you will be a lot wiser. If you do intend to manage the property yourself, though, there is a lot more learning to be done and you can find the main details summarised later in this book.

Chapter 8

How to grow your portfolio

There are several ways in which you can grow your portfolio from zero to whatever number you are aiming for. Initially, you may set yourself a target of buying three to five properties in addition to your own home as these are numbers that should yield a fairly healthy pension income. Your strategy will depend on the amount of time you have and how much control you have over your plan.

Things can control

- Your savings
- Your current property or properties
- The amount of time you stay in work (hopefully)
- Your finances
- Your spending
- Your strategy

Things you cannot control

- Life changes, e.g. illness
- Job changes, e.g. redundancy
- Your age
- The property cycle
- The economy
- Interest rates

Obviously, these lists are not exhaustive but I think it gives you the idea. The best thing you can do is continue to invest and save until there are changes to any of the uncontrollable factors in your life, but hopefully you will have more financial security than when you started out.

Be aware of the Property Cycle

While many people feel that property is a get rich quick scheme where they can make huge amounts of money in a short space of time, this is generally not the case. For most people and particularly landlords, property is part of a long term investment strategy and in order to buy and profit from property you will need to invest and hold over a period of time. This is similar to the stock market in many ways. If you want to make fast money then usually you need to take higher risks.

For the majority of people, we just want to invest, carry on with our lives and not have too much stress about the whole investment process. Consider this: when you invest in a work-based pension, you are not worrying or stressing about where your money is being invested or what the stock market is doing – although perhaps you should be!

The point is that if you are investing in property for pension you will need to have a different mind-set to property traders who want to make a lot of money. Investing in property is very profitable and if you buy at the right time when property moves into a fast growth part of the cycle then you can make money a lot quicker. For the majority of the time, though, property moves through the cycle in various phases. The beauty of the property cycle when looking at it historically is that property does continue to rise over time, although there will be times when it falls but it doesn't usually fall below the previous bottom which means that it is constantly rising. The stages of the property cycle include a steady phase, a stagnant phase, a growth phase and a rapid growth phase.

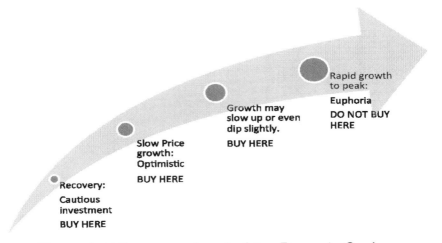

Figure 8.1 The upward part of the Property Cycle

The longest stage tends to be the slow, steady phase where there is slow but steady growth, sometimes a bit flat over a few years. It might be like the FTSE 100 where most of the shares are in big companies and so the price moves tend to be slow and steady without being overly dramatic for long periods, although they will be moving overall in an upwards or sideways direction. There is growth, your money is sitting in a nice profitable investment and you are happy to leave your money where it is.

At some period during this phase the market slows right down and may be relatively flat. Here, people stop buying with property being a bit harder to sell. Some investors may panic during this phase, particularly if they are over-leveraged in terms of borrowing and only just breaking even. At this time, they might think about getting out. For the majority, it is best to ride this time and stay put. When the market moves into a stagnating stage it stands still or starts to fall. There is often more panic at this stage but actually this might be the time for some investors to jump in and buy rather than trying to get out as long as they've not over invested during the growth period. It is also during this time there will be frightening headlines containing statements such as *property crash*, *property prices falling*, *and property no longer a good investment*. These headlines can induce fear and further panic. For the strong, well informed investor this is the time to see opportunity to buy as the prices will turn around again in the future.

If you can buy at the bottom of the cycle that's brilliant, but it cannot be predicted and it is more by luck than design if you manage to do this. It is better if you buy when you can afford to buy and if you do go into negative equity for a while by buying too soon, don't worry too much. For the majority of investors, they will wait for the recovery part of the cycle, so they are not buying at the bottom or while prices are still falling but when the market is turning around. This is the best time to buy as the market is shifting upwards and it is unlikely that property will ever be this low again. It is a safer time to buy as you know that prices are moving upwards.

If you do buy during this time, and buy one or two properties while prices are going up and up, it can be tempting to over buy when it might be better to hold and consolidate what you have bought. This will all depend upon the amount of risk you are willing to take. There will be a period of fast growth but at some point the cycle will readjust itself back into the slow and/or stagnant and falling stage of the cycle. Timing is everything in investment and greed can lead you down a slippery slope. If you can afford to invest and have plenty of spare cash, in some ways it doesn't matter so much as long as your costs are covered but why would anyone want to buy at the top of the market?

Personally, I would prefer to buy in the parts of the cycle that I have suggested in the diagram above because I like to feel safe and secure with my investments. You may decide that you have some risk money and are willing to use this at some stage to grow your money faster.

The cycle does repeat itself over 15- 20 years and property can double in price during that period of time.

Now let's look at the different strategies that can be used to grow a property portfolio. Some of them are similar to those used to get your first deposit. There are a number of ways to grow a portfolio and these include:

- Using your capital, e.g. savings, lump sums
- Developing partnerships with people you can trust to invest with
- Accumulation of capital in current portfolio & equity release
- Equity release from your own home

- Pension fund release
- Property trading to build up cash

There are different levels of risk to each of these strategies, but for any of them to work you need to ensure that you buy property at the right time.

Using Your Capital

The first thing to consider when considering growing your portfolio is that of using your own capital. This makes sense if you have saved or stored away cash to invest and investing this money in growing your portfolio seems like a good move. It is up to you how much money you are willing to put into property investment but you will need similar amounts to that of purchasing your first property as you are wanting to repeat this process.

Think about where you have money stashed away and what kinds of returns you are getting on that money. Some people have money in cash ISAs with very little interest and you may be one of these. You may, of course, prefer to leave that money tied up until interest rates rise as they should do over the next few years to get a better return. Do you have any other cash in savings accounts, long forgotten about?

One thing I would suggest is that you save from the word go, to grow your portfolio. In terms of savings accounts, compare the return on investment and yield with that of property. On average, you would be aiming for a minimum of 5% yield on property from rental income but your return on investment will be higher. See Chapter 8 for more information.

Always keep some cash aside for emergencies and have separate savings for those. Holidays and investments payments, for example, are often better kept in separate accounts so that you know what each pot of money is for.

You might be in a position where you have inherited a sum of money and it makes perfect sense to invest this in growing your portfolio once you have decided how much you want to spend immediately. Some people inherit a property and that is even better as you don't need to go through the purchasing process and you can add it to your portfolio. If it is a shared inheritance, consider buying the others out.

Ideally the property will be mortgage free although we will look at releasing equity in a short while.

You might be someone who is investing later in life, like I did, and you may have released a lump sum, taking advantage of the government's changes to pensions that allow you to release a lump sum at 55 years old. Before going to Vegas and spending the whole lot, it is definitely worth considering investing some or all of that money in property. You will still have control over the money and you are investing the money yourself with a greater sense of purpose which is very different to allowing fund managers to invest for you. Some people have released these lump sums and spent the money, not considering how they are going to live for the next 20-30 years. I am not criticising that approach, but it might be one that many regret as they get older. I certainly think that a portion of the money should be spent on something pleasurable but not all.

There are other ways of growing a portfolio with capital and this for you, might mean saving for the next one. Once you have saved enough money you can buy your next property. Some of the savings may have come from rental income from your first property and this is an ideal way to grow a portfolio because reinvesting is compounding and you will reap the rewards later.

Developing Partnerships

If you have a relationship partner, husband, wife, etc., then there are tax benefits from investing in property together as the tax burden will be shared. This can save you a lot of money in the long term, particularly since the changes in tax relief on interest only finance. It makes sense as you will be investing in a pension for both of you.

If you are not in that position or would prefer to invest with a business partner, friend or family member that too is a good way of building up a portfolio. It is a tried and tested method: lots of people invest this way. You do need to make sure that you are clear what happens to the property if you fall out or in the unfortunate case of one of you becoming seriously ill or dying. There are two ways to deal with this: when you purchase the property, a solicitor will ask you to make a declaration that your share in the property goes to your business partner or that it becomes part of your estate. For most people with families they will choose to have the share as part of their estate, but some people who have enough money elsewhere and don't want to leave their business partner in a mess choose the first method.

If investing with a family member, you will need clarity on whether you are sharing the ownership and responsibilities or whether it is a loan for you to grow your portfolio.

Accumulation of Capital in Current Property & Equity Release

By far the most common method that investors use is that of accumulation of capital in a current portfolio and equity release when that property comes up for remortgage (this is usually every two years, but it can be up to five if fixed). It depends on the amount of capital growth in that two year period, and that will depend on which part of the property cycle you are currently in. If there is a decent amount of growth you could have enough to invest in the next property, but if you are in a slower growth period you may want to wait four to six years before releasing the equity.

As I have already said, this is the most common way for investors to build a portfolio because it makes good sense to reinvest capital from your current investment rather than ploughing in more of your capital. There is nothing wrong with ploughing your own money into property if it helps you to grow to the number or properties that you want.

The way this type of equity release works is that your property comes up for remortgage and you apply to a different lender or the same lender for a different product. You work out how much you have already paid off if on a repayment mortgage and/or the amount of capital growth that has occurred since purchasing the property. You still need to leave 25% of the value in the property and you take out a 75% mortgage with the equity release being the difference between all of these figures.

Example

Purchase Price = £125,000
Amount borrowed @ 75% = £93,750
Amount of loan paid off = £1,800
Value of property now = £145,000
Deposit to be left in the property = £36,250

Amount of loan outstanding = £91,950

Loan required = £108,750

Equity release = £16,800

Remember that the mortgage payments will increase each month. This is why the majority of property investors opt for interest only mortgages in order to keep their repayments down. If you do not need to take any income out of the property other than for upkeep, bills and tax, and if your mortgage fits the lender's affordability criteria, there is no reason why you can't continue with repayment mortgages. If the figures are too tight, you would do well to opt for an interest only or part & part mortgage, and look to pay off lump sums when you have accumulated enough spare cash.

With the interest only method, you can usually build up your portfolio much quicker and switch to repayments once you have built up the portfolio you are aiming for. If you do not want the worry of the interest only, and if you want to be certain you are mortgage free at retirement, you can look at some of the other ways of building up a portfolio if the repayments are going to be too high from equity release.

Equity Release from Your own Home

There are a few different ways of releasing equity from your own home. The first one is that some people release equity from their home by effectively selling it to an investment company who give them the cash and allow them to live in the property until death. They use the money to enjoy or fund their retirement if they have not saved up enough to fund a pension. This is not the type of equity release that we are looking at here and this type of equity release makes me really sad.

The type of equity release we are talking about is that where your property has grown in value and you have a large amount of capital sitting in your home that you may want to consider releasing to invest in property. Personally, I would never release money from my own property to go on holiday or fund anything other than property investment. This to me doesn't make financial sense, but some people do this and they are perfectly happy doing it. In truth, I have not used this method but for some people it is an option that helps grow a portfolio a bit faster. In terms of the equity release we are talking, it is about investing and building a portfolio, and the only reason you would want to release equity from your own home in this case is to invest the money in another property or properties.

Do consider that your own mortgage repayments will increase, but if you are in a position where you are working and earning a good salary the costs may be easily absorbed into your monthly spend. The benefits are that you are now investing to build up your pension portfolio.

If you are anti this policy that is fine, you may be better off considering the other options discussed in this section.

Property Trading (Flipping) to build up Capital

There are a couple of ways to build capital. If you have a lump sum of around £50,000 but you want to build up your portfolio in a very short space of time, or the properties in your area require a much larger deposit than that, you can look at buying a property at auction somewhere in the country for £50,000 cash and then refurbish and/or renovate it.

You should get immediate capital growth and you can then sell it on. You can then use your profits to invest. The only thing you need to remember is that if you are selling to someone who needs a mortgage, you have to hold the property for at least six months as the purchaser will not be able to buy a property that hasn't been held for this length of time. If selling to a cash buyer, no problem. Some traders take out bridging loans which is another subject and you should take financial advice and research well before taking out a bridging loan. If the property is not mortgageable for any reason, you might want to consider a bridging loan.

Another way to do this is to still buy well below market value for whatever reason or at auction, but then use a mortgage for your purchase. Do exactly the same: renovate and refurbish, hold for six months and sell on. The only thing you need to keep in mind here is that most lenders charge penalties for mortgages that they offer at a discount, and so you may need to either pay these charges or opt for a mortgage that is variable for a term where there are no penalties. Ask your financial advisor or broker.

Also take into account that capital gains tax is payable on profits over £11,100 at present, so if you are going to make more money than this you will need to take this into account. If you invest with a relationship partner or family member then you both have a tax-free capital gains allowance of £11,100 or £22,200 between you so it would make sense when trading to use this allowance. If, however, you are selling to buy then you will not pay capital gains tax as you are still investing and not using the gains for personal use.

Many property traders do this for a living: buying and flipping houses without ever getting involved in buy-to-let at all, and some do a combination of both. Many property traders have become very rich from the process, but it is not without risk.

Property trading is a subject in itself and is not what this book is about, although you may want to use trading at some stage as part of your investment strategy.

Other

Some investors advise using credit cards and personal loans to help buy property, but it's something I would never do or advise. It obviously depends upon you, your circumstances and the level of risk you are willing to take or the situation in which you find yourself.

Take financial advice before embarking on any risky ways of borrowing.

Cash flow will be discussed in Chapter 8, but bear in mind that it is important to have a decent amount of cash to pay for any eventualities that crop up in the future.

Number of Properties

As discussed earlier in this book, the number of properties you will need very much depends on the amount of income you would like to have when you retire and when you want to give up work. For some people, three properties will be enough; for others, it might be four to six. In some parts of the country you can earn a very good income from one or two. There is no reason why you have to stop growing your portfolio at any of these numbers, but you can once you reach your target number. The number of properties also depends on where you live, what the yield is and on the return on investment.

The only thing would be not to try to grow faster than you can comfortably afford. Some investors in the past have over borrowed and ended up in trouble when the market dips. These investors tend to be the ones that hit the headlines in the doom and gloom periods. Also think of the fact that the tax burden increases when you have more properties, and you need to work out whether you are still in profit after tax and expenses. Nobody wants to invest in an unprofitable business. With the right approach, though, property delivers both short and long term profits. Remember to hold at various points in your portfolio growth, and if you grow and hold and grow and hold and grow and hold..... You will become a steady and wise investor.

Chapter 9

Tax & Accounting

In this chapter we will cover bookkeeping, accounts and tax responsibilities. There have been some far-reaching changes to taxation on buy-to-let properties that will be gradually phased in over the next four years and we have discussed these in earlier chapters.

Her Majesty's Revenue and Customs (HMRC) state that by 2020 they will be moving to a real time, online tax record for everyone and the annual tax return will no longer be required. Individuals such as landlords and businesses will need to report quarterly their profit and loss. This change is expected to come into effect for landlords in 2018, although the Chancellor gave a reprieve to small businesses in his recent budget. Whether landlords will benefit from this it is not clear. The majority of information about an individual will already be available to HMRC, but landlords will need to upload their profit and losses relating to property each quarter, which can be done by accountants. The changes are not yet intended to mean quarterly tax payments, but watch this space.

We know that Stamp Duty changes came into effect in 2016 and now apply to all second home purchases, including buy-to-let properties. This additional Stamp Duty also applies to holiday let properties and second homes. Capital Gains tax will apply to the sale of any second home, but Stamp Duty can be deducted at this time as it is classed as a capital expenditure. When maintaining your accounts, make sure that you keep records and receipts of any capital expenditure (this will be discussed in this chapter).

The first thing you must do when you start investing in buy-to-let property is to let HMRC know. If you don't, you will eventually be caught and since HMRC takes tax evasion very seriously you will be in trouble with a heavy fine and, in the worst case scenario, face imprisonment. If you are self employed or already fill out a tax return for other reasons, you just need to indicate this and complete the supplementary pages that you have other income from property. If you currently pay tax through an employer or fill out a paper return, you will need to inform HMRC that you are renting out property and they will send you a tax return to complete or the supplementary pages. It makes sense to pay an accountant to submit your tax returns, but you can do it yourself. HMRC is targeting landlords and actively seeking those who avoid paying their taxes. Theresa May made this clear in her first party conference speech as Prime Minister.

HMRC classes buy-to-let as a business, but there are some tax liability differences between trading as an individual/partnership and trading as a corporation. These will become clearer later. It is not too onerous to complete the tax form yourself, particularly if you only own one or two properties. If you are happy to keep up to date with what you are allowed to claim tax relief for then you may well be better off completing the return yourself. Tax frightens some people and if you are one, do yourself a favour and hire an accountant. Ideally, use an accountant who is familiar with property tax, especially now because of all the tax changes taking place for buy-to-let landlords. An accountant will probably save you more money than they charge over the long term.

KEY POINTS

- HMRC need to know about you
- Complete an annual tax return
- Find an accountant to do this for you if you do not want to do it yourself
- Keeping Records

You will need to set yourself up with an income and expenses ledger and keep all receipts relating to expenses. I use a spreadsheet in Excel. If you have an accountant they may provide you with a template to complete as it will help them as well as you. You can use a book or buy a ready-made ledger from a stationery supplier if you are not happy with computers. If you do like computers, you can buy purpose-built software for maintaining landlord accounts.

This is a list of the information you are likely to need and the headings they might come under:

- Rent, council tax, insurance
- Lighting, heating
- Repairs, maintenance
- Management fees
- Legal, professional fees
- Goods
- Miscellaneous

On a separate sheet keep a record of your loan interest as this will attract tax relief after net profit has been worked out from deductable expenses. If you intend to buy over the next few years take a look at my videos on Youtube that explain how to keep records up until 2020. After 2020 it becomes simpler although more expensive. If you are reading the paperback version of this book you can find the video links on the website http://www.buytoletinfo.com.

Ideally, you should open a separate bank account so that it is easier for you to see what is happening to your money and it also makes your business and personal finance easier to manage. HMRC can ask to see bank statements and a separate account is easier to inspect. A second bank account does not have to be a business account as these tend to incur higher charges. Any current account will do or even a savings account with easy access. You will need to keep all receipts and invoices relating to your property investment activities in order to claim as your records can be inspected at any time. If you are really busy in your day job, you can hire a book keeper to do this for you.

As you can see from the list above there are categories of expenses that attract tax relief. There are two separate records that need to be kept: one set for buy-to-let allowable expenses, which can be offset against profits, and capital expenses that are not claimable until you sell the property. It can be many years before you sell the property, so, as I said previously, make sure that your capital expenses are clearly recorded somewhere so that they can be deducted from any Capital Gains Tax further down the line.

KEY POINTS

- Register with HMRC if you do not already complete a tax return

- Inform HMRC of property income if you do already complete tax returns
- Keep a spreadsheet or a ledger for your income and expenditure
- Keep all receipts related to your property investment activities
- Keep separate sheets/records for capital expenses
- If needed, hire a bookkeeper and accountant
- Open a separate bank account – it does not need to be a business account

Annual Allowances

Annual Accounting for buy-to-let property works out as: *Property Income minus Allowable Expenses equals Taxable Profit, after this tax relief for mortgage interest attract is 20% phased for four years*

Allowable revenue expenses attracting annual tax relief

- Insurance costs (buildings insurance is mandatory if you have a mortgage), will also need contents if you let fully or partly furnished
- Heating and lighting for vacant property
- Advertising for new tenants
- Repairs and maintenance (can include tools if you do some repairs yourself, although larger tools will come under capital expenses)
- Replacement boiler (putting in a new boiler or central heating system after purchasing a property is classed as capital expenditure), replacing a boiler already in place is an allowable expense
- Research/training, e.g. buying books like this one, training courses, landlords certificates, if required (it has to be classed as improving a skill, so the definition can be a bit blurred. If you are a landlord already, books like this will come under this classification as will training courses and paid subscriptions to relevant organisations)
- Postage costs for sending letters to solicitors, agents or tenants

- Telephone calls relating to your buy-to-let business

- Legal and professional fees related to the tenancy, but not for property purchase (see capital gains section)

- Equipment – e.g. printing paper, ink cartridges, rent books, bulbs, smoke alarms, carbon monoxide detectors (check with an accountant or on the government website as some equipment for running business, e.g. a printer, is a capital expense)

- Letting agency fees includes every part of using a letting agent from advertising to full management

- Ground rents and service charges for leasehold properties

- Garden maintenance, gutter and drain clearances (comes under maintenance)

- Petrol, if you are using your car for travelling to and from rental properties

- Some home costs if running the business from home but check on HMRC website as to how to calculate. Alternatively, an accountant will do this for you. Remember to let your home insurer know if you are using your home for business. You will need to be managing a lot of properties to be able to claim as the rules relating to this changed in April 2013

- Bookkeeper fees
- Accountants' fees
- Refurbishment after the property is let that restores it to its original condition on letting
- License fees where a license is required to be a landlord

- Mortgage interest – 75% for 2017-2018, 50% for 2018-2019, 25% for 2019-2020 (see below)

Finance Now Separated and Calculated after Pre-Tax Profit Worked Out

Tax relief on finance mortgage costs has been changed to 20% and this is now calculated after pre-tax profits meaning that some landlords may move into higher rate tax bracket.

The relief is being phased in and tax relief at 20% will apply in the order listed below.

The rest of the finance costs for the relevant years is still offset against profit:

1. 2017-2018 25% of finance
2. 2018-2019 50% of finance
3. 2019-2020 75% of finance

The changes to tax relief shouldn't impact on the basic rate taxpayer, unless the change to the way it is calculated pushes you into the higher tax bracket. If you are a higher rate taxpayer, you will be paying more tax on property investments than previously. You will need to bear these costs in mind when setting and increasing rents as rent prices are predicted to increase as a direct result of these changes.

If you have recently seen in the news that rent prices have fallen due to a glut of properties, don't be discouraged. I believe this is what is classed as an 'outlier' in research terms. The increase in properties to let are mainly in London and the South East, and have come about from landlords over-purchasing in 2016 to avoid paying the additional Stamp Duty that came into effect from April that year. This will correct itself over the next twelve months as we still have a shortage of housing stock and an increase in people needing to rent.

You will need to keep in touch with what is happening on a regular basis through landlord forums and blogs. My website can be found at www.Buy to Let Info.com and there are many others such as Landlord Zone. If you are using a letting agent they should update you with any changes to legislation, as should your accountant if you have one.

The good news!

There are some tax benefits coming. The benefits are not directly related to buy-to-let property, but they will help you to pay less tax overall.

Personal Allowance & Higher Rate Threshold

This is the amount of money you can earn before paying tax and it will go up in April 2017 to £11,500 and in 2020 will increase to £12,500. By 2020, the higher rate tax threshold will also increase to £50,000 meaning that landlords with incomes less than that will not have to pay the higher rate tax.

The other good news is that, in spite of government promises to increase housing stock and help-to-buy schemes, there are just not enough houses and I believe the buy-to-let market will continue to benefit from this. Rents will increase as a result of the government's punitive measures on landlords. If you are careful about your investment portfolio and your cash flow, property remains a safe and exciting investment.

Losses Carried Forward

Another good thing about the buy-to-let business is that your losses are carried forward into future tax years and, as a beginner, you may not need to pay tax for two to three years because of your initial costs exceeding your rental gains. I built up my portfolio quite quickly which kept me from paying tax on my properties for the first three years.

Capital Expenses

Another government change is the loss of a wear and tear allowance. This was an annual allowance paid to landlords who let furnished properties. Replacement furniture and white goods can be claimed as a capital expense now, less any sale costs of that replaced. You need to keep all such receipts in a separate file or folder from your annual profit and loss account.

Legal fees and surveyor's costs cannot be deducted from rental income, but they can be deducted from capital gains when you come to sell the property. Legal fees related to property management, however, are deductible from your annual tax payment. Property improvements and refurbishment prior to rental also come under capital expenditure and are deductible on selling the property. Office furniture is classed as capital. As previously mentioned, it is important to keep notes and receipts for what you spend capital on as you will need these if and when you eventually sell the property, which can be years later. Tools and machinery used for maintenance also come under the heading of capital expenditure. A good accountant will add these to their records for use at a later date. Most of the money you spend on what is classed as capital expenditure will not be recouped for many years, so you need to keep this type of spending to a minimum.

The purchase price of the property is obviously the biggest capital expenditure and any profit in addition to the purchase price is liable to CGT, minus capital spending.

Example

Purchase Price = £120,000
Legal fees = £1,500
Capital spending refurbishment = £10,000
Stamp duty = £3,600
Survey = £150
Sale Price = £180,000
Profit = 180,000 – 120,000 – 1,500 - 10,000 – 3,600 - 150 = £44,750

Capital gains liability is £44,750, minus annual tax-free Capital Gains Allowance, (currently £11,300 per annum per person). It does change so you will need to check annually on the government website.

The annual tax free capital gains allowance will be deductible from the profit, but if you sell more than one property in a year you will only be able to claim it once. You cannot carry over the tax-free capital gains allowance into another year. If you have opted for a repayment mortgage and paid off £30,000 of capital this is not classed as capital gains and is not liable for tax. Capital gains tax only applies to the amount of profit over the purchase price.

Example

Purchase Price = £120,000
Capital paid off via Repayment mortgage = £70,000
Sale Price = £180,000
Capital gains tax only is only charged on the £60,000 and you can deduct the capital expenses listed in the previous example above.

Repayment mortgages for buy-to-let purposes tend to drain the rental profit, and this is why most professional investors opt for interest-only mortgages. HMRC will, and do, change the rules on capital and annual allowance expenses, so check with them and/or an accountant before claiming deductions.

If you hold property for life and then you pass it on as an inheritance, the people inheriting will not be liable for your CGT. They will, however, have to pay inheritance tax, which could be worse as it is charged at 40% once the deceased estate exceeds the allowance. You cannot gift the property as it would breach the 'gift with reservation of benefit' (GROB) regulations. You could either buy the property jointly with other family members initially or gift a younger relative cash to buy the property, as cash gifts are exempt from GROB, but you will need to live for seven years after gifting the cash for this purpose.

Capital Gains Tax (CGT) was reduced from 18% and 28% to 10% and 20% for most people, but, unfortunately, this change excludes residential property. The unwelcome impact of changes to CGT, however, is that the tax on residential property will need to be paid within thirty days of the sale of the property. It is likely that this will fall to solicitors to transfer this money around completion, as they currently do with Stamp Duty. Theoretically, however, you could hold the money for twenty-nine days to gain some interest.

KEY POINTS

- Keep separate records for allowable expenses and capital expenses
- Finance interest costs will no longer be classed as an allowable expense as such, but you will be able to claim 20% tax relief after profits have been calculated
- By 2020-2021 tax year, the only relief on finance will be 20%
- Start separating your finance interest costs in your accounting system to make it easier to calculate at the end of the year

Keep long-term records of capital expenses

Keep an eye on tax thresholds to keep yourself within the lower rate tax band if you fall into that at present.

Principle Private Residence (PPR) Exemptions

There are some rules that reduce the amount of Capital Gains Tax if you have owned a home, lived in it as a permanent place of residence, and then let it out later. These exemptions come under the Principle Private Residence (PPR) rules. You do not get CGT relief under the rules if you bought the house to make a gain. If you did buy the property as a home, and then later let it out when you moved rather than sell it as I recommended earlier in this book, you will benefit from these exemptions.

HMRC are clamping down on rogue PPR claims: you will need to provide evidence that you have indeed lived in the property or you will be refused the exemption. A number of cases have gone to court in recent years where landlords have tried to use PPR to avoid paying CGT. As soon as you try to claim PPR you will be on HMRC's radar.

There is a formula for working out how much PPR to claim. You are allowed an additional 18 months on top of the time you lived in the property which is classed as occupation.

The formula is:

Total capital gain x period of occupation ÷ total period of ownership

Example

House bought for £130,000 and sold for £180,000, Capital gain £50,000

House owned for 12 years = 144 months

Lived in by you for 8 years = 96 months

Deemed ownership = 18 months

Total Exemption period = 114 months

Total Capital Gain = £50,000

Exempt Gain £50,000 x 114 ÷ 144 = £39,583

Chargeable gain £50,000 - £39,583 = £10,417

In addition to PPR exemptions there is another tax benefit called Private Letting Relief (PLR). It can be a bit complicated, but you will not have to pay any CGT at all if the gain chargeable is below £40,000 because of PLR. In this example, the chargeable gain of £10,417 becomes exempt under PLR because it is less than £40,000 and so no CGT is due.

If the PPR gain had been greater than £40,000, you would have to pay CGT on the amount over that figure. These exemptions are a real plus for second residences or properties which you have held after moving and let out. If the property is jointly owned the PLR is per person and therefore doubled to £80,000: a very useful tax benefit. Do check with a tax specialist, accountant who is a property expert, or HMRC when calculating reliefs.

As I said before: don't try to claim PPR if you have not lived in the home as HMRC will be onto you in a flash. You will have to prove that you lived in the property as your main residence for a period of time and that you did not purchase the house for profit.

KEY POINTS

- Anyone claiming under PPR rules alerts HMRC to them, so don't try to claim unless you are actually entitled to the benefit
- These exemptions are great if you have lived in a property that you have let out as your CGT bill will be slashed

Stay up-to-date

Although I say you should get on with your life and forget about your properties until retirement, it is with the caveat that someone is keeping you up-to-date with legislation and regulation, especially as landlords are on the government radar at present. You could register with one of the landlord websites that send regular updates on any changes that are likely to affect you if you intend to manage the portfolio yourself. Also, check for yourself every so often and take a bit more notice of the Budgets and Autumn Statements. If you employ a letting agency, they should keep themselves and you up to speed with any new legislation, but you will need to occasionally make sure that they are doing what you pay them to do.

If you are going to manage your own properties, network with other landlords regularly. Get to know others in your area that are investing and meet up every so often. IFAs and brokers are a good source of information for changes in the way lenders are behaving and any further stringent rules they are likely to bring in. Keep an eye on inflation because you will know this will be a barometer for interest rate rises and you need to be forewarned.

Test your financial commitments every one to two years and make sure the properties are still working for you. Look at house prices to see where they are going. If you think you have over-borrowed, don't buy any more property at present: look at what you have got and whether an interest rate rise would cause you difficulty. If you plan well and stay on top of the market, you know you will gain in the long term.

If you intend to manage the properties for yourself, read Chapter 12. If you don't intend to do this, you can either skip it or read it so that you at least know what a letting agent should be doing. Over the next two chapters we will look at property as income and property for capital or lump sum.

Chapter 10

Property as Income

Although this book is principally about holding property for retirement, there will come a point when income is required. This may be at retirement or when a person wants to reduce their working hours.

Many people like to work, but there comes a time when quality of life outside of work becomes more of a priority and it is at these times when property income becomes a real bonus, even before retirement. Some people decide to give up the day job altogether and just concentrate on their property portfolio. Whether you develop the property bug or not, at some time you will want to retire and take a monthly income.

As I have said, many property investors have given up the day job entirely and taken on buy-to-let as a full or part time job. Even if you don't plan take any income from your investments until retirement, it is good to know that there is always that possibility. The term often used to work out whether property is a good investment, particularly on programmes like Homes under the Hammer, is rental yield. In addition to rental yield, it is important to think about return on investment (ROI) as it is this that makes property so exciting compared to investing in the stock market and other investments.

Yield

The important thing to note in terms of yield is that it should be positive and not negative. In other words, it should provide some cash flow at the end of each month. You should never be in a position where the property is costing you money to run − even during a downturn in the market, this should be avoided, if at all possible. If it does move into the negative, your asset has turned into a liability and, in such cases, it would be time to review your investment strategy. There would be various options open to you including:

- Selling some property/properties
- Changing from a repayment mortgage to an interest only or part & part
- Increasing rent/s
- Reducing your expenses
- Funding the losses yourself until the market moves upwards

Calculating yield will let you know whether the property is still making you money. This is not a once and for all calculation: your expenses may change if interest rates rise, for instance. You do need to do the initial calculation before buying property to make sure that the property you intend to buy is a viable option.

When you have planned well and monitored the property market, while keeping an eye on your accounts, you are unlikely to be taken by surprise if there is a property downturn and therefore you would have planned ahead.

There are two calculations to work out yield: one is for gross and one is for net. Often the examples given on the TV programmes are referring to gross yield and note they always say at the end subject to expenses.

Gross Yield

Annual Rental Income
———————————— x 100 = Yield
Purchase Price

Example

£7,140
——————— x 100 = 5.7% Gross Yield
£125,000

Net Yield

This takes into account the above plus expenses which include finance costs and annual operating costs.

Example

Purchase Price   125,000
Annual Rent   £7,140 (£595 per calendar month)
Mortgage Costs   £187 x 12 = £2,244
Annual expenses   £83.33 x 12 = £999.96
Letting Agent @ 9% £53.55 + VAT = £64.26 x 12 = £771.12
Total Expenses   £4,015.08
Total Net Income   £3,124.92

Net Yield

$$\frac{£3,124.92}{£125,000} \times 100 = 2.5\%$$

The annual running costs I have used have factored in one month void period and all other running costs. My actual running costs per property are less than £300 per year, but there is always a minimum amount kept in the account to pay for void periods of two months and a boiler replacement £2,000. I like to keep a minimum of £3,000 in each property account for these worst case scenarios so that I am not worried if a big bill comes in.

The net yield might be frighteningly low, which is often why people prefer to speak in terms of gross yield, but in this case it could still be a good investment because of the ROI shown below. Ideally, though, you want the net yield to be higher so that if your costs go up you will not get into trouble. Consider also that, even with a lowish net yield, these calculations are not taking into account Capital Gains Tax. You still end up with £3,124.94 profit before tax on just one average priced property. If you managed to purchase a property for below £100,000 with a similar rental income (not unrealistic), the net yield is much more attractive. The majority of investors are happy with a gross yield above 5%.

Return on Investment for Rental Income

Return on investment for rental income, as opposed to capital gains, is calculated by dividing the net yield by the amount invested (deposit) and multiplied by 100. You can add legal fees and Stamp Duty to the amount invested too, although these are capital expenses that can be claimed back on sale of property, and so I haven't included them.

Example

$$\frac{£3,124.92}{£31,250} \times 100 = 9.99\%$$

That's a 10% return on investment, which most people would be very happy with. I could have used a property purchased below £100,000 as an example, but you can do the sums for whatever priced property you like. When considering buying a property you should calculate for net as well as gross yield to check that you are going to end up with some cash flow at the end of each month.

Even though you may not be purchasing for rental income now, you still want to make sure that the property more than covers its costs. You can use your mortgage Agreement in Principle to deduct your mortgage costs prior to purchase and the expected rental income will be calculated from your research of the area. By doing these calculations prior to purchase, you will know if a property is a good investment or not. If the net yield is too low, look for different priced properties. If there are none in the area that you have decided upon, either look out of area or at different types of property.

Cash flow

Cash flow is really important for any business and property investment is no different. You need to be able to cope with the unforeseen. In order to sleep at night, it makes sense to ensure that you have enough spare cash in each property to deal with some of the more expensive emergencies, for example replacing a boiler or repairing a roof. You may never have to do either of these but have a contingency pot of money so that if problems do occur you are able to deal with them without taking money out of your own pocket.

Asset or Liability

An investment property is an asset for as long as it provides you with money in one way or another. If it starts to take money out of your pocket rather than fund itself, it becomes a liability and you would need to take another look at your strategy and/or portfolio.

I would expect my property portfolio to cover the following:

- Any finance taken out to purchase the property, e.g. mortgage repayments either interest free or repayment
- Costs of renting the property legally, e.g. gas safe certificates, licensing where relevant, buildings insurance and contents insurance where applicable
- Repairs and replacements required during letting plus expensive repairs
- Letting agents' fees, if used
- Void periods of 1-2 months
- Advertising prior to letting
- Tax bill relating to the property

- Personal expenses where applicable, e.g. stationery, petrol, tools, etc.
- Re-mortgaging fees

In addition, I would be expecting the property to be providing me with growth in the relevant bank balance if I am not taking an income from the property. Later on, it would need to provide me with an income in addition to all of the above.

Chapter 11

Property as a Lump Sum

Most pensions offer a lump sum payment on retirement. This is where property does differ slightly because pensions normally offer a 25% lump sum tax free. This can be really useful for investing in property or other assets, or for buying the dream car, going on the dream holiday or paying for kids through university. In the case of property, you have an annual tax free capital gains allowance which currently stands at £11,300 (and double that if you are a couple investing together). Any capital released after that, if not reinvested, is subject to Capital Gains Tax. There is a workaround and that is to release the allowance every year on each of your properties until you have the lump sum you require.

Workaround to gain benefits from Tax Free Allowance

Example

Year 1 - Property 1 – Remortgage – release £11,300 or £22,600 if you are a couple
Year 2 – Property 2 – Remortgage – release £11,300 or £22,600
Year 3 – Property 3 – Remortgage – release £11,300 or £22,600

If you only have three properties, you go back to remortgaging Property 1 again. You may not want to do this if you have paid all the mortgages off. In that case, if you want to release a lump sum, you would need to sell one of the properties and pay the Capital Gains Tax or remortgage the one property and pay the CGT.

Once you have the lump sum you need, you are able to do whatever you have planned to do with the money. You can start this process a few years before you plan to retire so that you have the same lump sum as if you had had it from a pension. Indeed, you might have a pension anyway and not need to do this, but the option is there for you.

Capital Growth

In addition to rental income discussed in the previous chapter, you should be expecting the property to provide capital growth over a period of time. Investors do not usually buy property just for capital growth, although sometimes you might while you are trying to expand a portfolio. Capital growth is often a by-product of investing in property over the long term. We have already said that property increases in value over time and that's what makes it so attractive. There are times when the growth is rapid, times when it is slow, and times when it is non-existent or even falling. Over time, though, the property will almost certainly be worth more than you paid for it.

When considering ROI in terms of capital growth it becomes really exciting compared to that of ROI from investing in the stock market due to leveraging, as we discussed in an earlier chapter. Be aware of Capital Gains Tax and how it applies to second homes. If you are unsure, take a look again at the chapter relating to tax and accounting.

If you do decide to sell a property do make sure that you claim all of the capital expenses that you shed out when purchasing the property so that you don't pay more than you owe. You can also deduct costs of sale of the property from the profit. Also, if you have ever lived in one of the properties yourself, you would be able to claim under PPR rules which can save you a fortune.

If you do end up paying capital gains tax, you will pay 18% as a basic rate taxpayer and 28% as a higher rate taxpayer.

Chapter 12

Letting & Managing the Property Yourself

In this chapter, we will discuss how to manage a buy-to-let property. Although some of this may not be relevant if you intend to use a letting agent for full management, you still need to be aware of your obligations in order to know what the agent should be doing. Also, the chapter will outline your legal responsibilities as a landlord.

Before advertising or even buying a property to let, you need to understand your responsibilities so that you are compliant with current regulations. Remember to keep up to date with any changes in legislation. This chapter will cover:

- Tenancy agreements
- Landlord's responsibilities
- How to rent – licences
- Finding a tenant
- Screening
- Moving in
- Managing the tenancy
- Dealing with problem tenants
- Ending the tenancy

Tenancy Agreements

A tenancy is a contract between a landlord and a tenant that allows the tenant to live in a property as long as they pay the rent and abide by the tenancy agreement that is in place. For the purposes of this chapter we will only be looking at Assured Shorthold Tenancy Agreements (ASTs), Statutory Periodic Tenancy, and Common Law Tenancies.

Assured Shorthold Tenancy Agreement (AST)

By far the most common tenancy agreement used now is the AST. Any tenancy that started from 28 February 1997 is classed as an AST even if there is no written tenancy agreement under the changes to the 1996 Housing Act.

The AST usually covers either a six or twelve month fixed period. Initially, you would only sign a tenant up for six months until you are sure they are right for you and right for your property. Under the terms of the AST, the tenant must not give notice until the tenancy is due to end and has to give one month's notice that would end on the final date of the tenancy agreement. Under Section 21 of the Housing Act 1988, you, as a landlord, have to give two months' notice and, again, cannot give notice until the AST is due to expire. This is called a Section 21 notice. The rules have changed with regards to landlords giving notice and enforcing eviction, so you should read the section on landlord responsibilities as you will not be able to give notice unless you have fully complied with the conditions marked with an asterisk. Also, read the section on ending a tenancy.

At the end of the AST term the tenants can either sign another AST for six to twelve months or move to a contractual periodic tenancy agreement which rolls over each month.

Example contracts can be found on various landlord websites, some of which you pay a subscription to join while others are free. You can also get a solicitor to draw one up for you, which is probably an unnecessary expense. I would recommend that you download the one from the government website to ensure that you are fully compliant with the most recent legislation. You can adapt it, but at least you will know that you have the most recent version. You can find a link to each of the relevant countries of the UK at http://www.buytoletinfo.com. If you are using an agent to find tenants or manage the tenancy, they will do this part for you. Ask for a copy of the AST so that you can familiarise yourself with the contents. This will help if you intend to self manage in the future.

If you were to buy a property with a sitting tenant, make sure that they have an AST rather than other tenancy agreements that may make it difficult for you to evict them if any problems occur. Personally, I prefer to find my own tenants who have been thoroughly screened.

Statutory Periodic Tenancy

This is a tenancy that is automatically entered into at the end of a fixed term AST which is not renewed. The tenant moves onto a monthly (can be weekly if rent is paid weekly) rolling contract and all of the terms and conditions set out in the AST still apply apart from the fixed term. You can increase the rent and change other terms and conditions during a periodic tenancy, following the correct procedure for doing so. Although these agreements might seem attractive they do not give you the security of knowing that the property is let for a period of time. Insurers prefer ASTs too.

Common Law Tenancies

These rentals shouldn't apply to you, but just in case you decide to go in for holiday letting, they are operated under common law rather than Housing statutes (although other laws may apply) and include:

- Holiday lets: a holiday let agreement is required

185

- Rent free or less than £250 p.a. or less than £1,000 p.a. in London: a non-assured tenancy agreement is required
- The rent is higher than £100,000 p.a.: a high rent agreement is required
- A company let: a company agreement is required

Landlord Responsibilities

Before the tenant moves in you will need to meet certain obligations that are required. Those marked with an asterisk must be supplied to the tenant prior to moving in if the tenancy started after 1 October 2015 and/or are obligatory. Without these, you will not be able to serve notice at any time until you are compliant. Landlord obligations include:

- Energy Performance Certificate*
- Annual gas safety check* by qualified Gas Safe registered engineer/plumber
- Electric safety check (advisory in all of England, Wales and Northern Ireland, compulsory in Scotland)
- Legionella safety check (risk assessment required)
- Smoke alarms (compulsory)

- Carbon monoxide alarms (compulsory in some properties)
- Government leaflet if AST renewed on or after 1 October 2015 for letting in England*
- A rental information pack must be given to tenants renting in Scotland*
- Registration/licensing under Rent Smart regulations if letting property in Wales*
- Registering deposit with an approved scheme*
- Check right of residency* (see under tenant checks)

Energy Performance Certificate (EPC)

An EPC must be available before you can market the property. A copy of this will need to be given to the tenant prior to the start of the tenancy. The certificates last for ten years at the time of writing. This is obligatory as you will not be able to give the tenant notice if you have not complied with this rule. You will need to purchase an EPC every ten years and provide the tenant with a copy. These are available online free if the property has been purchased recently, but will not be available if you have held the property for more than ten years.

Gas Safety

Every year, you are required to have each gas appliance, including flues, checked by a Gas Safe registered engineer/plumber. I always include a boiler service at the same time as it makes sense to keep the boiler in good condition. Once completed, the engineer will leave you and the tenant with a copy of a Gas Safety Certificate. The Gas Safety Certificate must include all gas appliances including boiler, gas hobs and gas fires.

You must give the tenant a copy of this before they move in if they are a new tenant under changes to regulations from October 2015. Please note that if you buy a property that has a building, such as a conservatory, off the kitchen where there is a gas hob and/or oven and the window opens into the conservatory rather than to the outside there needs to be some form of ventilation from the kitchen to the outside of the house otherwise the engineer can fail the property. Ask the Gas Safe engineer for advice, but usually an air brick will suffice.

Electrical Safety

Electrical safety is a legal obligation and the landlord is obliged to:

- Ensure that all electrical installations, such as sockets and light fittings, are safe before the tenants move in and are maintained as such
- You must also ensure that all electrical appliances supplied by you, such as cookers, have a CE marking

A periodic inspection and test is advisory and should be carried out by a Part P registered electrician every five years.

The test is legally required if the property is an HMO, but you can have it done anyway. I have all of my properties checked after I have bought them and then every five years. The electrician should give you a certificate on completion of any inspection

It is your responsibility to ensure that there are enough plug sockets in the property so that tenants do not overload plugs. If you buy an older property you will need to ensure the electrics are up to modern standards and that sockets are safe. A Part P registered electrician can advise and ensure the electrics are adequate for modern day living with computers, extra televisions, and so on. A common cause of fire is overloading of extension sockets.

Portable Appliance Tests (PAT) should be carried out on small electrical appliances that you supply but there is no specific guide on how often this should be carried out. A risk-based approach is recommended which usually means a visual inspection of leads and plugs. You should probably include photos that are dated and keep a record of the inspections.

Electrical tests became compulsory for all landlords in Scotland as of 1 December 2015, so it is important to check the legal requirements where you are buying property. In Scotland, the safety inspection consists of an Electrical Installation Report (EICR) and a Portable Appliance Test (PAT).

Fire Safety

As a landlord, you are obliged to follow safety regulations which include installing at least one smoke alarm on each floor of the property. The smoke alarm does not need to be hard wired, except in properties built after June 1992. At the start of the tenancy, it makes sense to change the batteries of smoke alarms and you must check they are working with the tenant. You will need to get the tenant to sign a form declaring that they will regularly check and change the batteries as required as part of their responsibility as a tenant. Advise the tenant to check the alarms monthly.

A carbon monoxide alarm has to be provided in rooms where there is an open fireplace that can be used or a wood burner. I provide these anyway and ask the tenant to sign a form accepting responsibility for checking and changing the batteries as required. As long as you follow the rules and supply them where obligatory you don't have to provide them for every property. Personally, I think it makes sense to provide them as it is likely they will become a compulsory obligation in the future. Follow the instructions on the alarms as to where they should be fitted.

If you provide furniture and furnishings, for example curtains or mattresses, they must have a fire safety label attached. You do not need to provide fire extinguishers or fire alarms unless the property is a large HMO.

Legionella Checks

Legionella is a bacterial infection that can cause a serious respiratory illness. The disease can be transmitted through water systems, particularly where there is stagnant water or water at temperatures between 20-40°C. There has been some confusion over the responsibilities of landlords in relation to Legionella safety checks. There has been no change in legislation regarding this but there has been a raising of awareness of landlords of legislation that covers Legionella risks.

The relevant legislation is the Health and Safety at Work Act 1974 and the Control of Substances Hazardous to Health Regulations 2002. These regulations require landlords to carry out a risk assessment around the spread of Legionella. A risk assessment does not need to be carried out by a professional but some plumbers are registered risk assessors. You as a landlord can carry out your own assessment and this includes:

- Ensuring the hot water temperature is set at 60° centigrade
- Ensuring any redundant pipe work is removed, e.g. hot supply no longer used for modern washing machines as water can stagnate and increase risk
- Ensuring that all water tanks have tight fitting lids to prevent debris entering the system
- Ensuring outside water taps have non-return valves to prevent backflow
- Regular flushing of system if property has been empty

If you are not happy to do this yourself, pay a competent professional to carry out the risk assessment for you. However you perform the risk assessment, you will need to keep a record of the check and any actions you have taken. Sign and date it with a witness present if you are doing it yourself.

Tenants' responsibilities

- Flush the system on return from holiday, particularly if there is a cold water tank but water can stagnate anywhere in the system so they should do it even if they have combi-boilers
- Regular cleaning and disinfecting of showerheads — probably the highest risk in domestic properties comes from showerheads so write this down somewhere for the tenant. Do it yourself in between tenancies

If you have a property that has air conditioning, this will need to be serviced regularly

Leaflets and Licenses

We have already discussed this in another chapter so please refer to that. You need to check with your local council in England if a landlord licensing scheme operates where you buy property for rent. Some HMOs in England must be licensed whether there is a general licensing scheme or not. In Wales, you will have to be registered as a landlord and licensed if you intend to manage the properties yourself. In Scotland, you need to register and licenses apply to all HMOs. In Northern Ireland, landlords have to be registered and there is a call for licensing.

Finding a tenant

Having read the rest of this book so far you will now have a good idea of your target tenant market. As part of your strategy you will know whether you are happy to rent to social security recipients, students, families, working people, etc. If you do decide to let property to unemployed people, students or people who have not recently rented or paid a mortgage similar to the rent price, you would be wise to request the tenants have a guarantor. The guarantor will need to complete a guarantor application form, and you should explain to them that they will be referenced and credit checked in the same way as the tenant.

You will now need to add some finer details relating to your preferred tenants. For example: are you happy to accept smoking in the property? Are you willing to allow pets? Be very specific if accepting pets as what you consider one small dog may mean a Rottweiler to someone else. If using an agent, they will generally state no pets in their advert or pets with agreement of landlord. If you totally exclude pets, you may limit your market as pets can be a part of people's lives. I own a dog, for instance. The balance is that pets can cause damage and some pet owners allow their animals everywhere.

If you are willing to accept pets on request, include a pet clause in the contract and request £100 extra as part of this clause for extra cleaning on vacation of property if required. Your agent, if used, will do this for you.

If you want to keep your friends and have good relationships with your relatives my advice would be: do not ever let to them. It is much harder to challenge a friend or relative over property maintenance than it is with someone who knows you are their landlord. Also, think about how comfortable you would feel about putting up the rent or dealing with complaints. It will be your property and up to you what you do with it but, personally, I would not go down this route and I think many other landlords agree with this principle.

Advertising

There are many people out there seeking rental properties, so once you know who you are looking for, state in your advert or through the agent the type of tenant you are seeking.

When advertising in a local paper be aware you will get calls from all sorts of people and they will not necessarily have considered your wording. Rather than waste time, as quite a few don't even turn up to view, arrange to be in the property for two hours on a certain day at a certain time and either give 10 minute appointments or let them turn up within that time frame. When they call you, ask them to bring ID with them on the viewing day to save you having to check this later.

You need to check that any tenant/s have a right to reside in the UK. This is now compulsory. You are obliged to check the documentation of each applicant face to face.

Personally, I have found newspaper ads to be more expensive than advertising on a property portal such as Rightmove. Let me clarify: as an independent landlord, you cannot go direct to the property portals yet but you can advertise on them via a company called Upad for a price.

Your property appears on all the major search engines just as if you were an agent and as most people search online nowadays you should get a lot of interest. You will need to take photos yourself and upload them. Make sure the photos show the property in its best light, including its strengths. You will need front and back plus photos of every room. I agreed to the let of one property within an hour of advertising on Rightmove via Upad after wasting money on a local newspaper ad and having a lot of time wasters view the property.

Screening

When a prospective tenant calls, ask a few screening questions. If you have said in your ad that you want working people, ask them what they do and where they work, also ask how long they have been there. Check about smoking, pets, etc. Ask who will be living there. Once you are satisfied that they meet your general criteria, let them have the address and viewing time, and remind them to bring two forms of ID and some cash for a holding deposit if they decide to apply, along with right to reside documentation if they are not from the UK.

Viewing

If carrying out the viewings yourself, make sure that someone knows that you are doing this just to be on the safe side and leave them with a list of prospective tenants' names and contact numbers.

On viewing day, you ideally want the prospective tenant to demonstrate they are responsible, firstly by showing up on time. Arrive early yourself and open all doors so that people can see the gardens and any outhouses. This also gives you more than one exit route if there are any problems. Make sure the house is warm if the viewing is being carried out in winter and open the windows if it is summer. You want to attract good tenants and show off the property as it would be if they were living there. Have information available for tenants that includes council tax costs, average household utility costs, whether there is satellite, cable TV access or availability, bus routes, local schools, shops, etc.

Have a few application forms with you so that if anyone shows an interest they can take them away to complete. You can either ask a solicitor to draw up forms for you or you can adapt them for free from websites such as *www.landlordzone.co.uk*. You can join as a landlord for free and download useful forms, as well as keeping up to date with new rules and regulations and events.

Ideally, by the end of a viewing timeframe, you will have an application and can proceed with the next step which includes credit checking and references. Request a holding deposit once a tenant confirms they would like to rent the property and give them a receipt for this. If letting to more than one adult they each need to complete an application form. One of the applicants will need to be the lead tenant, this is usually the person with the highest income. If you are requesting a guarantor, they will need to complete a guarantor application form. You will not usually request a guarantor for tenants who earn a good salary and who have been renting or paying a mortgage prior to the application.

References/Salary & Credit Checks
Salary

If you choose to rent to working people only, most letting agents require a minimum salary for one person or between them as a couple. If you are taking a tenant either employed or self employed, it would be in your interests to do the same. This minimum will be up to you to set, depending on the cost of rental, bills, etc. Sometimes a person may work just a few hours a week because they are sitting on cash. In some cases, as long as they can give a verifiable reason for the cash, an agent will request a full six months' rent in advance and, again, there is no reason why you should not do the same. If they want to continue renting at the end of the six months, you can do the same again. I have had one couple in this situation that had sold their home and not decided where to buy, so I had no problem renting to them for six months with the full six months paid in advance.

Referencing

If you are not using a letting agent at all, do take the time to collect two references with one being from an employer and the other from a previous landlord where applicable. You can pay a referencing or credit check company to do this for you. Many companies offer tenant verification checks.

In cases where the prospective tenant has not rented before you could obtain a reference from a previous employer or a character reference. For a self employed person, you should obtain a reference from a professional involved with them, e.g. accountant or lawyer. You could request references by fax, email or telephone as post tends to delay the process.

When referencing yourself, you will need to provide a questionnaire for the person to complete or a list of questions for them to answer. Ideally, you need to know how long the applicant has been known to the person. If employed for less than twelve months you should also get a reference from the previous employer. Ask whether the contract is temporary or permanent and the number of hours stated in the contract. A person on a 10-hour contract may be working a lot of overtime at present, but how long will this continue for and is it guaranteed overtime? Ask about severance and notice required to leave. If the applicant is self employed, do they hold insurance in the event of sickness or being short of work?

Credit Check

Prior to paying for a credit check you should ask the tenant to show you three months' worth of payslips and three months' bank statements. For a self employed person, you should ask to see 6-12 months' worth of bank statements. If you have not already asked for evidence of ID and proof of address you will also need to check these. The ID and proof of address items are the same as those used by banks and credit agencies:

- Photographic ID, e.g. passport or driving licence
- Proof of address ID, e.g. utility bill in the applicant's name or credit card bill

If the person is from outside the UK, you will need to see a visa or permit showing that they are eligible to work and reside in the country. You are legally obliged to ensure that people have a right to reside in the country before letting a property to them.

You will need to make copies of these records and keep them for one year after the tenancy has ended. Sensitive information should be stored securely.

There are a number of companies to choose from when carrying out a credit check. I use *www.tenantverify.co.uk* as they will allow landlords to use the service. They will also provide an application form with all the details they need to perform the check. A basic credit check costs around £17, inclusive of VAT. You can ask them to do the referencing as well as part of the check; this costs around £33, including VAT. I tend to do the referencing myself but use them for the credit check. There are other companies that will do the same thing for you. Of course, if you are using an agent to tenant find for you, this is all provided as part of the service.

Tenant Deposit Protection

Once you are satisfied you have the right tenant/s, you will provide a move-in date and request a deposit plus one month's rent in advance. I insist on a standing order to pay rent as part of the contract so that there are no misunderstandings about when rent is due.

If you are managing the tenancy, you need to register the deposit with a government approved deposit protection agency and this applies to the whole of the United Kingdom. For the most part they offer either a deposit scheme where you hand over the deposit (this service is free) or an insured scheme where you can keep hold of the deposit. There is a cost for the insured schemes where available and the deposit has to be re-insured each time you renew an Assured Shorthold Tenancy agreement which can be costly. If the tenant moves onto a Statutory Periodic Tenancy agreement the scheme will still insure the deposit for free. If you use a letting agent, they will also register the deposit with an approved scheme. You can find the relevant schemes on the government website – there are three for each country in the UK at present.

Whatever you do, if you do hold the deposit don't be tempted to borrow or spend it or you could end up in serious financial trouble when you need to return them. Also, be aware that if you are regularly renewing ASTs every six months, the fee for an insured deposit is chargeable again to protect the new agreement.

The tenant must be informed of which scheme they are covered by and the deposit has to be registered with one of the approved schemes within 30 days of taking it. You then have to provide the tenant with the information leaflet for the relevant scheme and a signed statutory information form. These forms are available from each of the deposit schemes discussed above. The company will also contact the tenant with details of the scheme and provide them with login details and passwords for themselves. If a tenant moves onto a periodical contract, you need to let the scheme know and they will continue to insure the deposit (usually at no extra cost).

Moving In

Before check-in day, ensure that the tenant signs for receipt of a gas safety certificate, energy performance certificate and government leaflet (England) or rental information pack (Scotland).

Information Pack

Provide the tenant with an information pack containing relevant information and include operating instructions for any appliances, central heating instructions or electric heaters if there is no central heating system. Instructions on how to light the boiler should be included. Other information to include:

- Local buses and bus routes
- Day/s the bins go out

- Local shops
- Emergency telephone numbers
- Location of water stopcock
- Location of gas mains switch
- Telephone numbers of electrician and plumber if you are happy for them to contact directly
- Signed inventory

When the tenant moves in there are a number of things you need to go through with them:

- Meter readings
- Inventory
- Emergency procedures
- Appliances
- Tenant responsibilities
- Contact numbers

You will need to write down all the meter readings; this usually includes gas, electricity and water (if there is a meter). If there is not a water meter installed in a property you buy and it is likely to be rented by one or two people it will save them money if you have one installed. This does not apply in Scotland; water charges are rolled into council tax payments and are not dealt with separately. The water companies will install them for free and it is a simple process. Having a water meter installed will also encourage your tenant to report a leaking overflow pipe sooner if they know they will be billed for the loss of water. You also need to let the tenant know which utility firms supply the property. The tenant should contact the firms with the readings, but I always do this as well as it is not unusual to get a bill a month or two down the line if the tenant hasn't done this for themselves. The same applies to council tax. The tenant will be responsible for arranging telephone, broadband and extra television services from an independent supplier.

Inventory

By necessity, you should always have an inventory for the property and include photographs. If there is any dispute over damage at the end of the tenancy you will have evidence of the original condition. Minor damage and repairs are easily rectified, but more extensive damage can be costly. Damage caused by the tenant or their family, visitors or pets is their responsibility. Losses and breakages are also the tenant's responsibility. If you don't want to do this for yourself, you can hire an agent to let the property, create an inventory, screen tenants and do the check-in. They can then hand the property back over to you to manage.

Emergency Procedures

You should let the tenant know how to vacate the property in an emergency (for example, a fire). There should be an exit both upstairs and downstairs allowing escape.
Guidance on what to do if the tenant smells gas or suspects a leak should be given, and they should know how to turn off the gas supply in an emergency. Make sure the tenants have a key to the gas and electric meter cupboards if they are located outside the house.

Advise the tenant that water leaks should be reported immediately and show the tenant where the mains stopcock is so they can switch the water off. Water leaks are costly and there is usually an excess on the buildings insurance due to this being a relatively common occurrence in rental properties. If there are individual stop valves for pipes, such as sinks, baths and toilets, explain how these can be turned off while still allowing a water supply to the rest of the property. The tenant should also report leaking overflow pipes where they are fitted.

Drain problems should be reported to the water authority if the problem is with the mains drain. Other drain problems will be the responsibility of the landlord and the tenant should report any blockages or smells.

Gutters and drainpipes can become blocked with leaves in the autumn causing overflows that can damage brickwork, so ask the tenant to report any overflow from gutters and it will be your responsibility to get them cleared.

You should advise the tenants that they should not allow electrical appliances, such as washing machines, tumble dryers and dishwashers, to run when they are not at home due to the risk of fire.

Ask the tenants to air bathrooms regularly, and if the bath or shower sealant is becoming loose to report it as soon as possible. The most common problem I have come across is water leaking through ceilings due to bath sealant coming away from the wall. The tenants continue to shower and cause the problem to become increasingly worse. This is a costly problem. The damage caused by the spread of water can leave you with a hefty bill. Always inspect the bathroom when you do your regular checks. Better to pay for a bit of sealant replacement than redecoration when the downstairs ceiling is stained or may even need re-plastering if the damage is severe. You can probably tell, I am talking from experience here.

Visiting the Property

Before visiting the property for any reason, except in an emergency, you must give a minimum of 24 hours' notice. This is because the tenant has rights from the AST. Remember that while they have an AST agreement in place, it is their home. If you do not give notice the tenant can report you to the local authority. Try to give as much notice as possible before carrying out inspections or visiting for routine repairs.

Tenant's responsibilities

The tenant should:

- Pay the rent on time even if in dispute with you (I insist on a standing order). If you are renting to people on benefits they will usually pay the rent to you, but some councils will pay the rent directly to you and deduct from benefits
- Take good care of the property, report any problems and pay for repairs where they, or their family or friends, have caused the damage
- Turn cold water off at the mains if they are away during cold weather
- Leave some central heating on low or frost setting on boiler if they are away in cold weather
- Pay utility bills and council tax if this is in the tenancy agreement
- Not sublet the property without permission
- Not keep pets, except by agreement
- Not do anything illegal or allow anything illegal to go on in the property

- Not use the property in a way that would cause a nuisance to neighbours
- Not alter the property without permission. If you want to keep tenants and allow them to feel at home, it is worth letting them do some decorating and put things on the walls as long as they make good on vacating the property
- Not change the locks

The tenancy agreement will include a list of other things that the tenant should and should not do, but these are the main ones. It is up to you whether you allow smoking in the property but, if not, it should be made clear before the tenancy and in the AST agreement. Wear and tear is your responsibility so you cannot charge the tenant for this. Most good landlords will decorate or have the property decorated every five to eight years.

Minimising Void Periods

The best advice I can give is: be a good landlord or landlady. If you treat the tenant with respect and keep the property in good repair, acting promptly when there are problems, this will be to your mutual benefit. Obviously not all tenants will be good tenants, but the best way to avoid these is to do all the screening you can before ever letting them inside your property. There are lots of people looking to rent property and if you have bought in the right area and present a property in good repair you can afford to be choosy.

There will be some areas where there are more properties than tenants and these can be a little harder to let. In these cases, you might want to spend a little more time and money to make the property a bit more 'high end' than other properties in the area. You may also consider letting to tenants on benefits in these areas as they tend to be more long-term renters. Of course, there may be problems with this if the tenants decide to spend their benefits on things other than rent, and you may want them to have a guarantor prior to renting who would be responsible for paying the rent if they don't.

Allow tenants to feel at home. If they want to decorate or upgrade the property, let them as long as they understand they need to leave any replacement carpets or other items when they vacate the property. They could put the old ones back down but there aren't many tenants who would want to store old carpets!

Not every tenant understands reasonable decoration, so you will need to stipulate that colours should be neutral or you may be shocked to find a black bedroom. At the end of the day, you want the tenant to be happy and to feel that they are at home. If you are too strict about what they can and cannot do they may never settle and are more likely to move on.

There are some provisos: for instance, if you know a tenant is only going to be in the property for six months, you would not want them to make any major changes unless it is going to benefit the property for the next let. Be reasonable but not gullible, and aim for win-win tenancies wherever possible.

Increasing Rent

The Assured Shorthold Tenancy agreement should have a clause that will either state that the rent is fixed for a period or that it will be reviewed at regular intervals. If there is no mention of reviews in the AST and tenant does not agree to an increase in rent you need to wait until the agreement ends before increasing the rent.

If the agreement is a contractual periodic tenancy agreement it will need to state how often the rent will be reviewed.
If you do decide to increase the rent, you should write to the tenant giving them notice of the amount of the increase and when it will start.

You can use a formal procedure to propose rent increases at yearly intervals under the Housing Act 1988. There is a formal procedure for proposing a rent increase if it is not covered by your contractual agreement where you will need to use a special form which can be downloaded at *www.gov.uk* and it is called: *'Landlord's Notice proposing a new rent under an Assured Periodic Tenancy of Premises situated in England'*. The form is not required if your tenancy agreement already contains a clause about rental increases. You can increase the rent at the end of a fixed term AST but you should still follow the correct procedure and give the tenant notice.

The tenant can disagree with a rent increase, in which case they need to apply to the Residential Property Tribunal

(RPT) who will review the proposal and decide what the rent should be. You cannot appeal against their decision.

You can usually come to an amicable agreement regarding rent increases, in which case there will be no issues. I usually wait until near the end of an AST agreement and review every two years, but it will depend on your circumstances and what is happening in the economy as to when you decide to increase rent. Once interest rates start to rise and the changes to tax relief start to bite there is no doubt that rents will increase yearly and that they will spike over the next five years. Because of the changes to tax legislation, I will be increasing rents for all of my properties at the end of their next AST agreement.

Nuisance Tenants

If your screening process is thorough you should be able to minimise or even exclude nuisance tenants totally from your properties.

The vast majority of tenants do not create problems for you or for others. Some tenancies can, however, become sour.

Your target market, by its very nature, may be more prone to nuisance tenants and you will need to bear this in mind if you undertake the higher risk types of letting, for example students. It does not necessarily mean that all students or tenants on benefits will create problems, but the risks are higher than average. Marriage breakups and domestic violence affect every aspect of society and you will need to be aware that this could happen. It will also depend on where your property is located and this is why some local authorities have introduced licenses for landlords where there are more likely to be problems with antisocial behaviour. These licenses mean that if there are a number of complaints, the landlord can be contacted and will be held responsible. Licenses have already been discussed.

The most common form of nuisance is that of noise, particularly in the case of young people or people who are at home all day because they don't go out to work. Complaints will come from neighbours and if this occurs, it is usually enough to give a soft warning, explaining that it is unreasonable to disturb neighbours with loud music, televisions or parties. Most tenants will respond to this and curb their behaviour, or at least reduce the length of time they play loud music. Most neighbours will put up with a bit of noise, but they will be on your back if it is constant.

You should carry out regular inspections, particularly in the first six months of a tenancy. Most agents do them every three months. I do them shortly after move in and then every three months. For my long-term tenants, I combine inspections with renewal of contracts or maintenance calls. The inspection lets you know that the tenants are looking after the property and not causing any damage. If there is a lot of damage you will need to let them know they will be liable for repairs and reiterate the contractual agreement to look after the property.

It is very common for tenants not to look after gardens and you can request that they do this regularly. If necessary, provide a few tools or you can join the many landlords who pay a gardener to regularly maintain the gardens, particularly at the end of a tenancy. I personally believe it is the tenant's responsibility. As they know this, the garden is often maintained just prior to one of my inspection visits. If you are using an agent and there are frequent comments in their inspection reports about the garden being in a poor state of repair, remind them of their responsibilities to manage the tenancy. When I used a management agent this was one of the things I had to get onto them about. If you allow the agent to do as little as possible, some of them will. If you do use an agent, you will need to manage them as well — don't forget they are working for you.

Missed rent

In most cases, rent should never be missed if you insist on a standing order or direct debit, but if you choose a different method of rental payment, such as a weekly or monthly rent book then this could happen. However you collect your rent, you need to be on the alert for any missed payments. If the tenant contacts you and explains for some genuine reason that the payment may be late, it is up to you how flexible you want to be. Overall, though, this could be opening up the door to problems further down the line. A tenant who is going to become unemployed should know well in advance unless he/she has been made redundant due to an unexpected company closure. Likewise, students whose loans are late should be able to at least give you a date when they are expected. If a tenant gives you no warning at all and does not pay the rent, you will need to contact them quickly.

If personal problems mean that a tenant requests leaving before the end of the tenancy, it is probably better for you to let them go but explain that you will re-advertise while they are in the property if it is in a reasonable state. If it is not, wait until they leave but explain they must leave the property in a good state of repair or their deposit will be at risk.

Ending the Tenancy

When an AST is coming to an end you can give the tenant at least two months' notice to quit the property. This is known as a Section 21 notice. You may not give notice to quit before the end of the AST. If you are giving two months' notice, the date of the end of the notice should be the date of the end of the tenancy agreement. Under the Deregulation Act 2015, if the tenancy started after October 2015, you must issue a no fault possession order by completing Tenancy form 6a available from *www.gov.uk*. In order to serve notice you must have complied with all the relevant legislation pertaining to renting a property mentioned in the landlord's responsibilities section.

If you have not complied with the rules discussed earlier you will not be able to operate under Section 21 of the Housing Act 1988. If you have complied and in the unlikely event that the tenant does not move out after you have served the notice on the date required, you need to apply to the court for a possession order. You can apply for an accelerated possession for a fee without a court hearing. See _www.gov.uk_ for details. Most tenants leave following a Section 21 (form 6a) request if you need your property back at the end of the AST agreement and, as mentioned before, if your vetting process is good, you will be highly unlikely to have to deal with any problems.

There are provisions under the Deregulation Act 2015 that prevent you from serving a Section 21 notice for tenancies that started on or after 1 October 2015 and the notice will be invalid if all of the following provisions are met:

- The tenant has complained about the state of repair of the property and the landlord fails to provide an adequate response within 14 days of receipt of their complaint
- The tenant then complains about the same issue to the Local Authority

- The landlord's response to the tenant's complaint was to serve a Section 21 notice

The Local Authority will serve the landlord with a notice of improvement or emergency action and the landlord cannot serve a Section 21 notice again for another six months.

Section 8 Notice

A Section 8 Notice applies to tenants in breach of one or more terms of the tenancy. There are eight mandatory and nine discretionary grounds for you to re-possess a property which you can find at *www.gov.uk*.

A Section 8 Notice is a last resort, a tenant may need to be evicted for non rental payments but this is not a simple process—you can't just tell them to leave or send in the bailiffs! The rent arrears need to be for more than two months (if rent paid monthly); you then serve a Section 8 notice. You still need to have complied with the statutory obligations already mentioned. In this case, you can give between two weeks' and two months' notice. See the Government website for further details of when this Notice applies. The form can be downloaded at *www.gov.uk/guidance/assured-tenancy-forms#form-3*. You may need to apply to court for a possession order as detailed above if the tenant does not leave by the date specified in the notice.

Checking Out a Tenant

Once the move out date has arrived you or your agent will need to check the tenant out by comparing the property before and after the tenancy. This is where it is important to have a detailed inventory. Ideally, you check out with the tenant and you need to ensure all keys are returned. It is not unusual for tenants to have extra sets of keys cut, so do request these as well. Some landlords replace locks at the end of tenancies, but in most cases this is not necessary (except in the case of eviction where you may want to consider this option).

Once you have checked the property, you should agree with the tenant if any money is required from their deposit. If you disagree, you will need to apply to the deposit protection scheme with which you have covered the deposit for a resolution of any dispute. The decision of the deposit protection scheme is final and once this has been agreed you must return the remaining deposit to the tenant if you are holding it. If the Scheme is holding it for you they will pay both you and the tenant the agreed amounts.

Read the meters with the tenant where possible, or as soon as they have vacated the property, and let the relevant utility companies know who is now responsible for bills (which may be you or a new tenant). Also, let the local authority know for council tax purposes. Make sure the tenant knows to cancel any cable or satellite television services. Ask the tenant for a forwarding address to send on bills or post. Most tenants will arrange for a Royal Mail forwarding service for a few months, but some post does tend to slip through.

Once all this is done, you are ready for the next tenant. Hopefully you will have advertised the property during the notice period and will have a new tenant lined up. If you haven't been able to arrange viewings due to problems with the property or the tenant, book them for as soon as possible after the tenant has vacated. Every day the property is empty costs money, but you already know that. If any re-decoration is required, book the tradesman in for the tenant's move out day or as soon after as possible. Some tenants won't mind moving in while the place is being spruced up, while some would prefer to wait.

Tenancies and repeat tenancies should run as smoothly as possible, and if you are paying an agent make sure they are aware that you expect seamless transitions wherever possible with no long void periods.

Chapter 13

Letting Agents

Although I have already covered some aspects of using letting agents, I thought it would be useful to add some extra information with regards to employing an agent.

If you want to be completely hands-off then you will need to hire the services of a letting agent. If you intend to manage properties yourself but would like someone else to advertise & screen the prospective tenants you can use an agent for this purpose too. Letting agents come in all shapes and sizes, from one-man bands to large national names and everything in-between.

It is important that you find an agent that you can trust to do their job so that you can be stress free once the property is let and leave it in their hands. Personally, I would go with a letting agent only who doesn't deal with sales because where they deal with both, the lettings side tends to be seen as the less attractive side of the business.

I have personal experience of this as I used a sole letting agent to manage my portfolio and they did an excellent job – until the day they moved into sales. The company expanded and whilst I do not begrudge them this, the lettings side of the business went by the wayside. Instead of being able to relax as I had done before, the whole lettings side of the company became shambolic. This was such a marked contrast to how the business was before that I moved my properties away from them. Other landlords I met with agreed that the same problems occurred and I have found that whenever there is dual registration the lettings side tends to underperform. I realise I am generalising here and that you may have a different experience, in which case, I wish you well.

There are two letting agent associations that a letting agent can register with, neither is compulsory. These are:

- Association of Residential Letting Agents (ARLA)
- National Approved Letting Scheme (NALS)

ARLA seems to be widely respected and some lenders insist on an ARLA agent's rental estimation as part of their application. It doesn't mean you have to let through that agent but you will need them to assess the property and provide you with a written rental estimate. Being registered means that the agent has to comply with the rules of the organisation and inspections can be carried out periodically.

Services that letting agents offer vary as do their charges. Ideally find an agent that advertises transparent charges with 'no hidden extras', particularly when using an agent for full management as some will charge to renew the tenancy every six months even for the same tenant.

Services offered by letting agents are:

- Tenant finding – some include check-in free as part of this service
- Tenant finding plus inventory
- Partial management

- Full management

Tenant Finding

For an agreed fee, the agent will advertise the property, find a suitable tenant, verify their identity, reference and credit check them. Some agents will check the tenant in as part of this service and others will charge an additional fee of around £25.

Tenant finding fees vary from a fixed fee of around £300 to £400 to a percentage of the first month's rent. For example they may charge 50 – 75% of the first month's rent. An inventory will cost extra at around £100. From 2018, tenants will no longer be charged application fees due to government intervention outlined in the autumn statement of 2016, and these may be passed on to landlords.

The agent would also be responsible for verifying your identity as a landlord.

Partial Management

Prices vary for this service so you will need to check with your local letting agents. This service would include the above and some additional extras:

- Registering the deposit with an approved deposit protection scheme
- Collect rent and pass on to you after deducting the agent's commission
- Arrange annual gas safety check
- Send you monthly statements
- Deal with the check out of tenant
- Negotiate deposit release

Full Management

This would cost a fixed fee and an additional monthly charge of between 8 to 12% of monthly rental plus VAT so you will need to negotiate right from the start. The figure advertised does not have to be paid and I have found that most agents will move on price. The full management service includes everything above and the following:

- Advice on your legal obligations
- Referencing and credit checking guarantors where appropriate
- Preparation & signing of tenancy agreements
- Giving tenant details of services & utilities including council tax details
- Reading meters at check in
- Production of inventory
- Collecting rent & passing on to landlord minus commission
- Monthly statements
- Property inspections and reports
- Arranging for repairs & maintenance, instructing tradesmen
- Dealing with tenants for breach of terms, rental arrears etc
- Advising landlord if legal action needs to be taken
- Checking out tenants
- Re-letting property

Conclusion

Using the right letting agent will save you a lot of stress and if you are time poor, then a full management service might be what you need. When looking for an agent, do your research and approach it from an employer's perspective. You are hiring them to do a job and you need to be able to trust them to do it professionally & efficiently. If they cannot, then do not hire them.

Chapter 14

Holiday Lets

Firstly I will hold my hands up and admit that holiday letting is not my area of expertise but it would be remiss of me not to mention it as it is popular and can be very lucrative. Overseas holiday letting is beyond the scope of this book so will not be discussed here. The main advantages to buying a holiday property to let in the UK are:

- High yields because property is let on a weekly basis
- No evictions or long-term problem tenants to deal with
- Payment in advance

- Generally less wear & tear and damage charged to person renting
- Adds diversity to portfolio
- Can be bought cheaply because they do not have to be in thriving cities or towns
- Can use for yourself, family & friends

Yields

Because properties are let on a weekly basis the yields average out at much higher rates than ordinary buy-to-let properties. The average charge per week is four times the usual monthly rent for a similar property in the area where you are letting. Obviously you need to ensure the property is let.

No Evictions

People visit properties for a holiday and therefore there is no risk of people staying when they are not supposed to. They will leave at the end of their tenure and go home. Even if you have people staying who cause problems, they are there for a short length of time.

Payment in Advance

People pay for their holiday in advance.

Wear & Tear

If there is any damage to the property, it is paid for by the person renting for the holiday. Wear & tear can be less than average because people tend to go out when they are on holiday. If you accept pets you will be able to charge the extra amount for the extra cleaning required in-between lets.

Spreads risk

Adds diversity to your portfolio and people will always go on holiday.

Purchase Price

Many properties bought for holiday lets can be lower in price with less competition because they may not be in the centre of towns. They are more likely to be in the country or near a beach or place of interest. Some areas such as Devon though will be very expensive to buy holiday properties in due to the popularity of the destination. The returns though would also be higher.

Occupancy

Peak periods will usually be fully booked but you will need to include focussed marketing on the other months. Good marketing is key, be available and friendly if you are not using a management company. Develop a good website to advertise the property. If you are not great at website development you can outsource this task to an organisation such as Fiverr.

Private Use

You & your family or friends can stay in the property when it is not let. Not always in the peak season and a management agent will expect you to let the property in peak seasons although they usually allow you a few weeks I am told.

The main disadvantages are:

- Set-up costs higher
- Seasonal occupancy
- Takes more work

Set-up Costs

The property needs to be fully furnished and contain everything a family needs for the period of time they are on holiday. This would include appliances and a television at minimum with many including DVD players, dishwashers and other high end appliances and gadgets. More & more holiday lets' are including Wi Fi as part of the deal. Insurance will be higher for holiday lets and you will need a specialist mortgage. If you can afford a cash purchase, this is an area of the market where it would be worth buying in cash.

Seasonal

Mostly the occupancy is seasonal and you may encounter problems getting it let out for the amount of time that you need to in order to make a profit. Good marketing can overcome this though and many people make a very good living from holiday letting.

More Work

Generally a lot of time has to be spent marketing the property and it can be a specialist area. There are letting organisations that specialise in letting holiday properties.

Conclusion

Many people successfully invest in holiday lets and can make a lot more money from doing so than in the usual buy-to-let market. If it is done properly and with the right amount of research, it can be a very profitable investment. Stamp duty for second homes does apply to holiday lets and will need to be factored in to purchase price. Tax advice will need to be sought from a tax advisor specialising in holiday letting.

Chapter 15

Buy, Hold, Rinse & Repeat, Retire

Throughout this book, I have tried to maintain that in order to invest in property for a pension you will find it much less stressful if you buy, hold, let, buy, hold let, etc. For some people who start early enough and who have a good work income, they will be able to do this and distance themselves completely from their property portfolio once it is at the stage they want it to be. For others, this may not be part of the strategy. You may want to buy and hold and either reduce your working hours or manage your properties and make that your job.

Many people enter into the property investment market, mid-life because other expenses and priorities have taken hold prior to this and it is often when kids have grown up and left home that there is more free income. It really doesn't matter at what age you start, as long as you have a strategy that eventually provides you with a decent retirement income so that you can do all the things that you want to do with your retirement.

Once you do make the decision to retire it is time to re-evaluate your portfolio and your responsibilities. Just like anyone who is about to retire, you will want to know what income your properties are going to generate and also to decide whether you want or need to take a lump sum out of your investments. If your properties are fully paid off then you have a guaranteed income for life and you can even put up the rents every so often as the market allows.

If the properties are not fully paid off, you will need to determine whether the income they are generating is enough for you to live on or whether you still need more properties or whether you need to sell any either to release capital for you to spend, trade more properties or to pay off the mortgages.

There is no reason why you cannot continue with interest only mortgages but you may want to take advantage of hot periods of the property cycle to pay off lump sums and reduce the overall burden. At some stage, if you have mortgages, you will reach an age where lender are no longer happy to extend the loans and at this point you will need to consider what you want to do with them. There are a number of options:

- Sell enough properties to pay of mortgages on the rest and keep those without loans
- Gift the properties to your children/other, passing on the loans to them (you would need to involve a solicitor)
- Sell them all and live off the proceeds (subject to capital gains tax)

It is up to you whether you continue to manage the properties yourself. Many people do this as it keeps them active and interested. If you do want to retire completely, though, hand them over to a letting agent so that you can forget about them.

Conclusion

I hope that this book has provided you with some valuable information that will spur you on as you seek to fund your retirement through a buy to let property pension. There are many advantages to investing in property as I hope you have seen through reading this book. It is now time for you to take action if it is an area that you would be happy to invest in. Many people, including myself have had to start somewhere and buying the first property is usually the biggest hurdle.

You will notice that I haven't discussed downturns in any great detail and this is because if you invest sensibly and well within your means, you should, on the whole be able to hold property through changes in market conditions. Do evaluate and re-evaluate your portfolio though when the market does change and particularly if money is becoming too tight. You should not need to fund your up and running portfolio out of your own pocket and if this does happen you will need to take steps to prevent future losses.

On a positive note, historically property prices do increase and are likely to do so in the future. Do remember though that past profits, are not a guarantee so always keep your portfolio in check and if sales need to be made then so be it.

I wish you every success with you future investments.

Claim Your *FREE* Bonus

As a thank you for reading this book, I have put together a bonus for you to claim for FREE. Sign up by clicking on the link below to gain instant access to the bonus at: http://www.buytoletinfo.com/property-hotspots/

Bonus

Quick-start Guide to UK hotspots for buy to let property in 2017

This report looks at a number of property hotspots with thriving buy to let investment areas throughout the United Kingdom. Included in the report is an area for speculative investment.

To access the report for free please go to http://www.buytoletinfo.com/property-hotspots/

Password to access: Bonus

Useful Links

Accountants

www.accountant-directory.co.uk

Blog

www.blog.buytoletinfo.com

Credit Referencing

www.clearscore.com

www.equifax.co.uk

www.experian.co.uk

Deposit Protection Schemes

www.depositprotection.com

www.mydeposits.co.uk

www.tenancydepositscheme.com

www.mydepositsscotland.co.uk

www.safedepositsscotland.com

www.lettingprotectionscotland.com

www.lettingprotectionni.com

www.tdsnorthernireland.com

www.mydepositsni.co.uk

Government Websites

www.gov.uk (with rental re-directs across the UK)

Insurance

www.buytoletinfo.com

Landlord Websites

http://www.buytoletinfo.com/

www.landlordzone.co.uk

www.thepropertyhub.net

www.landlords.org.uk

www.rla.org.uk

www.scottishlandlords.com (Scotland)

www.landlords.wales (Wales)

www.lani.org.uk (Northern Ireland)

www.upad.co.uk

Money Information/Research

www.moneysupermarket.com

www.moneysavingexpert.com

www.thisismoney.co.uk

www.money.co.uk

Pensions Information

http://www.ageuk.org.uk/money-matters/pensions/changes-to-state-pension-age/

https://www.gov.uk/browse/working/state-pension

https://www.pensionsadvisoryservice.org.uk/

Postcode Area Information

www.crimestatistics.co.uk (crime)

www.streetcheck.co.uk (demographics)

http://www.neighbourhood.statistics.gov.uk/dissemination/ (demographics)

www.homecheck.co.uk (risk reports subsidence, radon, coal mining, landfill, historical land use, pollution)

www.environment-agency.gov.uk (look up flood areas)

Price Comparison websites

www.gocompare.com

www.comparethemarket.com

www.moneysupermarket.com

www.confused.com

www.uswitch.com

www.which.co.uk

Property Websites

www.rightmove.co.uk

www.zoopla.co.uk

www.nethouseprices.com

www.mouseprice.com

Rental Information Available to Tenants

www.citizensadvice.org.uk

www.shelter.org.uk

Tax

www.hmrc.gov.uk

www.gov.uk

YouTube Channel

www.buyto.letinfo.com

Dear Reader

I hope you have enjoyed this book and that it has provided you with enough information to either keep you investing in property or help you make a start. I would love it if you could leave an honest book review on Amazon and any social media platform that you may use. I value the opinions of readers and will read every review.

If you would like to keep up-to-date with all things property then please subscribe to my website at www.buytoletinfo.com and YouTube channel. I also have a property blog (www.blog.buytoletinfo.com) and aim to write at least once a week on all things property.

Please share with friends and family and I wish you every success in your property investment endeavours for the future and cheers to your eventual retirement.

Other Books by Dawn Brookes

Business/Property

Buy to Let: 7 steps to successful investing

Memoirs

Hurry up Nurse! Memoirs of nurse training in the 1970s

Hurry up Nurse 2: London calling

Health Books

How to check blood sugar

Appendix Checklist for Purchasing Buy-to-let Property

How much can I afford to put down?

What would I like to buy – house ☐ flat ☐ Maisonette ☐

How Many bedrooms? 1 ☐ 2☐ 3☐ More than 3 ☐

How do I want to buy? Estate agent ☐ Auction ☐ Leaflet drop ☐

Where can I afford to buy? Close to home ☐ Same town/city ☐ Within 50 miles ☐ Further than 50 miles ☐

Have I narrowed down the area? Yes ☐ No ☐

Start looking within price range +/- £10,000 ☐
Make a shortlist for viewing: Property addresses, date of viewing ☐

Start viewing ☐

Have I got a solicitor in place? Name, email, contact ☐

Do I have an agreement in principle for a set amount? ☐

Make a second shortlist after viewings ☐

Pros & cons list ☐

Rental estimate – estimate yield ☐

Is the price negotiable? Yes ☐ No ☐

Is the property a good investment? Yes ☐ No ☐ Potentially ☐

Make offer ☐

If rejected, go to number two on the list ☐

Offer accepted ☐

Will there be any refurbishment required? Yes ☐ No ☐

Estimate cost of refurbishment ☐

Estimated time to completion: Known ☐ Unknown ☐
Leave solicitors, agents & lender to do their work unless going too slow ☐

Appoint an agent if using ☐
When near exchange of contracts date start putting feelers out for tenants ☐

Advertise property on exchange of contracts ☐

Completion date – viewings ☐

Agree tenancy with agent if using and leave alone ☐

Get on with life ☐

Start the process again until portfolio target reached ☐

Dawn Brookes Publishing
www.dawnbrookespublishing.com
www.buytoletinfo.com

22154124R00149

Printed in Great Britain
by Amazon